A Benedictine Soul

A Benedictine Soul

Dom Pius de Hemptinne, Disciple of Blessed Columba Marmion

Biography, Letters, & Spiritual Writings

THE CENACLE PRESS
AT SILVERSTREAM PRIORY

First published in French as *Une Ame Bénédictine: Dom Pie de Hemptinne, Moine de l'abbaye de Maredsous*, this edition is based on the 1935 English version of Sands & Co., translated by the Benedictines of Teignmouth, published as *A Disciple of Dom Marmion: Dom Pius de Hemptinne, Letters and Spiritual Writings*.

This edition republished 2022 by Silverstream Priory with the kind permission of Maredsous Abbey. Minor errors have been corrected and slight adjustment to typographical styles have been incorporated into this edition. New material and graphic design copyright © 2022 by Silverstream Priory.

All reservable rights reserved.

The Cenacle Press at Silverstream Priory
Silverstream Priory
Stamullen, County Meath, K32 T189, Ireland

www.cenaclepress.com

Nihil Obstat: Censores deputati.
Imprimire Licet: +Caelestinus, *abbas* Maretiolo, 5 jun. 1935.
Imprimatur: P. Cawet, *Episc. coadj.* Namurci, 21 jun. 1935.

ppr 978-1-915544-07-0
cloth 978-1-915544-08-7

Typesetting by Nora Malone
Cover design by Silverstream Priory

Contents

Preface to the First Edition • vii
Preface to the 8th Edition • xi

I. Biographical Sketch
Introduction • 5
I. Which Draws the Portrait of the Youth • 13
II. The Vocation • 21
III. The Novitiate • 29
IV. The Years of Study of Theology • 41
V. He Studies Theology • 59
VI. The Teaching Monk • 73
VII. The Final Grace • 89

II. Aspirations and Thoughts • 109

III. God's Note Book • 171

IV. Selected Letters • 217

V. Thoughts and Letters of Dom Pius • 261

Appendix I • 267
Appendix II • 269

Preface to the First Edition

*There are hidden flowers that no one sees,
and which perfume the whole air, from their little
cups. Such, also, are certain souls. All who approach
fall under the charm of their virtues, most of all,
that delightful sweetness which is the true fragrance
of holy souls and the good odour of Jesus-Christ.*

—From the "Thoughts" of Dom Pius, CIV

This volume contains the private spiritual notes and some extracts from the letters of a monk of the Abbey of Maredsous, Dom Pius de Hemptinne, who died on January 27, 1907, aged twenty-seven years.

The humble life of this young religious was marked by no brilliant action, nor by any mystical phenomena calculated to attract attention from the crowd.

Even within his own monastery Dom Pius did not hold any important office: he was just a simple monk, and distinguished only for the perfection of his ordinary life: he knew how to obey and how to love. All his greatness lay in that—there lay the secret of the divine fragrance which perfumes his memory and which may still be found in his unpretentious writings.

Dom Pius left two Journals —daybooks of his own spiritual life, written down day by day, as he was led by circumstances and the inspirations of grace.

These run on parallel lines, but bear a very different stamp, one from the other.

The "Aspirations and Thoughts" are the result of experiences of monastic life: Dom Pius writes simply of events as they occur, reasons about them, and draws, in his prayer, teachings as a general deduction from them. From thence, the direction, being impersonal, veils, or scarcely veils a warm and living reality.

Although these "Thoughts" are detached from each other and seem to stand singly, yet all form one perfectly homogeneous whole: one great thought pervading and giving a strong cohesion to the entire collection.

The sanctuary of Dom Pius' soul is opened to us in "God's Notebook." By the secret communings of the religious we are introduced to a sphere that is entirely mystical. He never showed his "Note-book" to anyone, and it was only found after his death. Here the heart speaks, alone with its Beloved, "never wearying of repeating: the same thing." ("God's Note-book," *Aug. 4, 1904*.)

The worldly-minded could never understand or enter into these things, but the initiated will know how to appreciate the charming freedom, they will be able to value the simple and true accents of a powerful love.

A few "Selected Letters" show us the ascetic principles to which Dom Pius constantly returned as the key to perfection. Here we find the monk in contact with others and he shows himself to be no misanthrope. The correspondence kindly communicated to us by friends is comparatively voluminous; more than four hundred letters having come to our hands.

Preface to the First Edition

Those who seek to penetrate the true sense of the religious life; and in particular of the Benedictine spirit will, we believe, read these pages with interest: and, in fact, they lay open with touching sincerity, that which passes in the soul of a generous monk.

These various writings belong only to the last seven years of Dom Pius' life and furnish few details. In order to help the reader to follow the work of grace in that monastic career, a "Biographical Sketch" has been placed at the beginning of this edition which may be omitted, if preferred, should the reader's time be limited.

—Dom John de Hemptinne

Preface to the 8th Edition

The eminent qualities of doctrinal science and ascetical experience of the distinguished author of *Christ the life of the soul, Christ in His mysteries,* and *Christ the ideal of the Monk* are widely known and the masterly manner in which he has treated of the most delicate questions in the spiritual life.[1]

In the autograph letters addressed by the Sovereign Pontiff Benedict XV to Dom Marmion, he deigns to say that "he had himself gone through the works in so far as his occupations had allowed, recognising their singular aptitude to excite and foster the fire of divine love in hearts: (*noticing also*) how well the doctrine therein put forth with regard to Jesus-Christ as being the Model and Cause of all sanctity, is capable of inflaming souls with the ambition of imitating

---

[1] "*Le Christ, vie de l'âme*" is the finest spiritual work that has appeared in recent years…"*Le Christ, idéal du moine,*" is worthy of its precursor… The unanimous welcome given by the Catholic world is a just proof that the Abbot of Maredsous is counted among the masters of spiritual doctrine. The theological solidity, the understanding of souls, and the exact simplicity of expression, ensure the lasting success of these works. Appreciation of human needs, and the unction of the Holy Spirit are the secret and the guarantee of prolonged fruitfulness." R. P. Doncœur, S. J., *Études*. See also Dom R. Thibaut, *Un maître de la vie spirituelle, Dom Columba Marmion,* 25th thousand.

Him, and with ardent desire of living by Him, Who has been made, by God Himself, our Wisdom, our Justice, our Sanctification, and our Redemption."[2]

Witness from so august a source suffices by itself to recommend a doctrine. But, nevertheless, it would be very fitting to see the doctrine fully set forth before us in a concrete existence. And this is exactly the case and in a remarkable way in Dom Pius de Hemptinne. The characteristic of that young disciple of Dom Marmion was, in fact, an immense love for God, going so far as to make a total gift of himself, even as an un-limited sacrifice, even to the joyful acceptance of all suffering. As he himself says: "The reason why man was created, is that he may love. His only need, his sole strength, and his joy is to love. But it is to love You, o my God, that man was created—that he exists: the need that presses him is the want of your love: his sole strength, the way in which he becomes strong, is in loving you: the rest which he finds in you, alone gives him true joy. Thus, he never ceases his search, until he finds himself lost in you forever: oh! increated Love!"

This thought of Dom Pius' at once penetrates his whole life and explains it.

※

Now, as we shall see in Chapter IV, it was to Dom Marmion that Dom Pius owed the "Revelation of love." "The wings of his soul, which had, hitherto, been folded, now spread open to their full extent, and that bold flight of the young monk's spiritual life began which, in the short time of seven years soared through the regions of divine love, and carried him to heaven."[3]

---

[2] Letter of October 10, 1919. This letter refers only to the two first works; the third having not at that date been published.

[3] Monseigneur Schyrgens, in *Revue Generale*, February 1923.

Preface to the 8th Edition

It is true that, when Dom Marmion undertook the direction of this soul, no one of his books had yet been published: *Le Christ, vie de l'âme* did not see the light until twenty years later.[4] But from the year 1900, Dom Marmion had been in full possession of his ascetical doctrine, and the Conferences given by him in the Retreat of 1900 contained the very kernel which was drawn out in the first of his works. *A disciple of Dom Marmion* (une ame bénédictine)" thus constitutes a "proof of before letters" of the *Christ the life of the soul*, and also gives a most striking and touching illustration of Dom Marmion's doctrine....[5] Dom Pius had perfectly understood and lived the "Mystery of Christ," as he had received it from the teaching of Dom Marmion that the young monk's soul became able to leave us the admirable spectacle of such sure and rapid mounting towards God.

In order to understand the interior life of Dom Pius it is necessary to study that of his "father in Christ, who brought him forth in Christ," and unveil the essential ties which united him with the author of "*Christ, the life of the soul.*" To see, in fact, from what pure sources the disciple drank abundantly of living water, and thus be better able to grasp the causes of the powerful fecundity of that short existence.

At the crossing of the paths of the spiritual life, Providence arranged that Dom Pius and Dom Marmion should meet: their names, like their souls, must ever remain inseparable.

---

[4] *Christ the Life of the soul*, appeared in 1918; *Christ in His Mysteries*, 1919; *Christ the ideal of the Monk*, 1922.

[5] The day after the death of Dom Marmion it was most truly written: "If Dom Marmion had done nothing else than give a saint to the cloister, it would have been enough to glorify him. In reality, Dom Pie was the living commentary of "*Christ, the life of the soul,*" and "*Christ, the ideal of the monk,*" those two fine works of his full maturity. But his chief masterpiece, Dom Pie, is known by the intimate and personal notes which he left, which display the posthumous revelation of his hidden heroism." —Monseigneur Schyrgens: *as above.*

A Benedictine Soul

In October 1922, the Abbey of Maredsous celebrated its fiftieth year of existence. At the fraternal *agapes* which followed the religious ceremonies, His Eminence Cardinal Mercier, recalling the past of the monastery referred to the memory of certain souls who had embalmed the Maredsous cloister with the perfume of their virtues. Among these, the heroic Prelate distinguished "the *angelic*" face of Dom Pius, and declared, before the numerous assembly, that his cause deserved to be introduced at Rome.

The value of this opinion from such lips can easily be understood.

A Benedictine Soul

I

Biographical Sketch

I should like to write the history of my soul, because this would be to the glorification of Thy merciful goodness, oh! my Jesus, and to the humiliation of a soul that is unworthy of Thy predilection.

—From "God's Note-book," June 23, 1908

Introduction
The Inheritance

Be ye faithful to God.

In the good old days, when home influences were strongly marked, a certain stamp was impressed on character, as it were by birth, together with a full heritage of faith and of ancestral virtues.

Ah! who can worthily describe that homely atmosphere which endowed us with so much besides our life-blood!

However, the individualistic and anæmic order of things in our own times has not so utterly enfeebled the family spirit that it may not sometimes retain and hand on some hereditary treasure, without suffering it altogether to escape.

And thus it was that Yvan de Hemptinne, the Dom Pius of later years, was endowed in his very cradle with a jewel of inestimable worth. This jewel was neither sword nor toga, nor the gift of a writer's genius; but it was the Evangelical Pearl of great price, the purest of supernatural ideals.

Let us but open the Memoirs of his grandmother, who noted in her Journal many little deeds and words of her children; those thousand *nothings* which tell us so much.

It happened, she tells us, that one day the children were discussing a grave question—no less than to decide which of them was the luckiest? "I am!" cried one of the little boys, "I am—for I am to have an operation in my ear: it is to be lanced, and I can suffer for God!" The others, who did not look forward to the privilege of a surgical operation, found this argument conclusive. The greatest good fortune —the best luck—was his, clearly, who had a chance to suffer something for the love of God. The principle being accepted, the application followed as a matter of course. This good Mother was once hesitating as to which of two remedies should be applied. "Give me the nastiest," said the little sufferer, "because, today I want to bear something for the conversion of sinners, the perseverance of the just, and the consolation of all in trouble." These were such good reasons, concluded the mother, that I yielded to his wish.

Sometimes this "good zeal" went a little too far, as we read in the "Journal".—"This morning X. came to me with his hand in a bandage, and on my asking him why it was so, he replied that the nurse had done it up like that. "That is all very well," said I, "but Janet would not have done that to amuse herself! What silly thing have you been doing?"—"Oh! no, Mama," he replied, half laughing and half ashamed, "I sawed off the skin with my saw, to see whether I should be brave enough for martyrdom." This did not chime in with Mama's good sense, and, perhaps half unwillingly, she gave the flayed martyr a good rating. But, this valiant woman knew by her own experience the joys of mortification, and practised penances which her children still recall with veneration.

With regard to worldly amusement, all were alike condemned and despised with equal feelings of disgust and reprobation: on this point there was no "beating about the bush." It was enough that Christ had censured luxury and vain pleasures. Therefore, every true follower of Him must break with the world. This austere and generous line of

Introduction

conduct had been adopted in the spirit of a deep love of God, and was followed with the uncompromising force of a faith truly Roman.

One little instance, taken from the same Memoirs will show how far abnegation was practiced.

"During the Easter holidays of 1864, fearing lest the light music so fashionable then, should be harmful to my dear children, I asked them to limit themselves in future to music of a style fitted to elevate their souls, as religious music does, instead of such as softens and enervates them. To dear M. this was a real trial. She loved music, and could not make up her mind to part with a number of operatic pieces which I regretted having ever allowed her to play. She protested, and, for the first time was unwilling to do as I wished. I was heart-broken at giving her so much pain, and would gladly have endured far more myself to spare her; but I felt it my duty to insist, and nothing could dissuade me. In a few hours the dear child had calmed down, and she said no more about it. I comforted her as well as I could by undertaking to pay for the lodging of a poor girl whom M. visited and was interested in. This offer on my part made her quite happy again."

It was in this way the supernatural joy of a good deed obliterated the sensuous charms of worldly music in a young girl of eighteen.

The poor people of the neighbourhood flocked around this truly Christian hearth, attracted by the warmth of charity, and they always found a hearty welcome.

Before the children could speak plainly, they held out their little hands full of gifts to the needy. To quote again from the *Journal*: "X., from the time she was quite tiny, was easily moved by anyone in trouble. One day, a poor mother came asking me for some warm stockings for her child who was barefoot. X., who could not talk yet, began directly to pull off her socks, and, when I asked her what she did that for, she pointed to the woman, and made signs to show me she wanted to give them to her. I began to put on her socks again,

A Benedictine Soul

but she would not have it and began to cry bitterly until she had been allowed to give the beggar some warm, thick little stockings."

Joys, new-year gifts, little savings—all these went to the poor, and any one of the children taken by their mother to visit the cottagers, was considered lucky indeed! "This," says the Journal, "was the most welcome treat I could offer." In preparation for these visits, all cakes or sweets were hoarded up, and it was the children's delight to share them with their dear poor."

Thirty years passed: one of these children, after having been a member of the Corps of Papal Zouaves, set up a home of his own: and in that home Yvan was destined to be born. Here was the same supernatural atmosphere, here were the same principles and the same ideals as in the preceding generation, but with a certain distinctive tone which should be noticed, for it is found reflected in Yvan's soul.

The home life had become more familiar in character, perhaps a trifle less austere, but perfumed with a closer fraternal intimacy. Under an outward appearance of almost child-like simplicity was hidden that best spirit of Christianity, a solid union of hearts, one deep aspiration of the soul towards God, common to each member of the family, but in a way that is incomprehensible to the worldly-minded.

A large circle of ten children surrounded their parents: eight sons first appeared, and then, to complete the garland, two daughters were born.

In order to bring up this goodly company well, the family mansion became quite an educational establishment. The father and mother were so devoted to their children's welfare that they renounced all social engagements and gave themselves up completely to fostering the growth and development of their beloved young people. This was their greatest pleasure. Of course, the task was a difficult and complicated one, but far harder would it have been to send their children away from them, to school. Partings must befall—soon enough—and to

Introduction

let such young birds fly from the nest would be to expose them to forgetfulness of the principles that would be needed to strengthen their wings in later life.

The morning and evening gatherings of this happy little community were pervaded by joy and frank cordiality. After Mass, which was celebrated in the house chapel, the family met at breakfast, the children kissing their parents lovingly, and then begging their blessing. On each forehead the father's hand traced a little Cross as he said the words "God protect and bless you, dear child." Then there was a rush to the fire to toast their bread, each hoping for the golden crust of the round loaf. Thus, amidst laughter and love they lived under a cloudless sky with hearts that were ever light and free from care.

At the appointed time, the Chaplain who was also tutor, gave the sign to proceed to study, and a thunderous glance—on any laggard on the way upstairs to lessons. After a well-filled day, the whole family met again, and spent a delightful evening together.

The joys of the paternal hearth are never to be forgotten; many years later, Yvan received a letter recalling this happiness in moving terms:

> If the bitterness of breaking up the family circle wears off a little with time, affection keeps all those closely united who made part of such a family circle as ours was. What a home! All the roots of our life have taken shape in that frank friendship, happiness, piety and courage. Home! sweet home! There, where others have had little, we received abundantly. It is not to be wondered at that these precious years are unforgettable, and that time only adds sweetness to the memory!...But, *there!* I'm getting sentimental and had better take my temperature!

All this frank union and spirit of family life had deep roots in a lively piety which was not limited to prayers said in common, nor even to the habit of frequent Communion. The religious spirit among these good souls had an almost contemplative bent. A wee tot said, innocently, "the most cunning are those who only love God."

A strong light will be thrown on this interior life by a letter which it will be well to quote in this place, although it was written to Yvan when he was just entering religion. It shows the hearty conviction of a Christian mother:

> My very dear child,
>
> During these days, when you are preparing to offer the full sacrifice of yourself to Jesus-Christ, my heart does not suffer me to keep silence: my thoughts fly constantly to you, and, although it is a sacrifice (and one keenly felt) for us to deprive ourselves forever of your presence with us on earth, though it is a sacrifice to our hearts—yet, above all this, in the superior part of the soul there is great sweetness and consolation.
>
> How often do I not pray to God to establish you in this region of peace, of light and of love, where you will be truly pleasing to Him, and where you will also find true happiness! How often do I not thank God for having deigned to choose some of my children and drawn them to live in the pure air of religious life, away from the miry paths of the world! The evil one will sometimes try to present to your imagination those joys and delights that you have renounced: send him off, boldly and with the scorn that he deserves: for nothing in the whole world can be compared with the joys of divine love. Is it not evident that the Author of all things must Himself be delightful beyond any of them? And is it not more justice to devote our soul to its Creator, rather than to any of His creatures?... to the supreme and initial Beauty, rather than to any of the broken rays that emanate from Him?
>
> The nearer you draw to It, the more in love with It you will be—but on condition that you guard your soul, and keep it pure from all that displeases God. If your soul be penetrated by the Divine Light, like a beautiful crystal that is exposed to the beams of the sun: away from the divine rays the soul is dark, without beauty or radiance.

Introduction

And what can I say?—what can I ask from God for you, my very dear child, more than this—that you may live forever in that Light and that Love?

On the other hand, the more austere voice of the father does not falter in wishing that his sons may suffer—for suffering is the necessary way that leads to sanctity. He wrote to them:

If a tear must flow from your eyes, I pray that our dear Mother, the holy Virgin Mary may gather it up as it falls and offer it Herself to her Divine Son. After earth's sorrows will come eternal bliss.

We may mention here, that, though Yvan never knew his grandmother from whose *Journal* we have quoted, yet he owed much to the influence of his grandfather whom he tenderly loved. Children and grandchildren gathered round the venerable old man, whose chief joy lay in instilling into the rising generation the love of holy Church, hatred of the Revolution and of liberalism—in a word, all the *good old* principles!

※

Such were the patriarchal surroundings of Yvan's childhood and boyhood which form the natural framework to his character.

Chapter I

Which Draws the Portrait of the Youth

A loveless nature is like a sunless spring.

—"Thoughts" XXX

The portrait of Yvan de Hemptinne at eighteen sums up his childhood, and foreshadows his future. He was now a tall youth, and had the happy gift of an even temper. In his whole appearance shone a purity and elevated look which was at once charming and apt to inspire respect. His unaffected and frank manner was marked by gentle gravity, whilst his broad shoulders and brow gave the impression of a determined character and an iron will. This energetic firmness, however, was tempered by extreme sensibility which inclined him to an excessive reserve. The contour of his mouth expressed kindness, but his look was too innocent to invite caressing affection, and in the limpid depths of his eyes a fiery soul dwelt hidden.

Moreover, Yvan's heart was governed by strong good sense and a well-balanced judgment which protected him from the surprises of sentimentality. His intelligence being solid and a little slow, did not lend itself to pure abstraction, the part of that faculty being to open out vast horizons to the loving soul. If he felt this need for a "general idea" it was not so much because he had a taste for speculation, as because of the unbounded largeness of his soul. The mysterious floated around him, intangible but none the less real; he felt himself penetrated by large conceptions and ardent aspirations, often without clear outlines. These conceptions and aspirations were such as a calm imagination loves to clothe with ornaments drawn from the marvels of God's creation.

Better than all this, a certain rectitude of will characterised Yvan at this time; a decided bent towards the supreme good. His soul was naturally drawn towards God, and was exercised by a thirst for the Infinite. Even before his birth, his mother had made an offering of him to God; not only as she had offered all her children, but in a very special way, begging the Lord to make this little one "a very privileged soul," and she prayed "deign, oh! my God, to make known the wonders of Thy grace and Thy holy love in this little soul." At his Baptism she gave him the names of "John Benedict"[6]; not that these names were traditional in the family, nor from any special circumstance, but her choice was fully justified by after events. From that time, no doubt, the apostle of love lighted a spark of divine love in his little namesake's soul, a spark which the holy Patriarch of monks fostered and sheltered under his cowl.

※

Whilst still very young indeed, Yvan had, as it were intuition of supernatural things: he spoke of God with surprising ease, and was full of grief when he examined his conscience, to find that he loved anything except for the glory of God. He earnestly tried to become better, although, in the path of perfection he found, "one climbs up very slowly."

---

[6] The Russian form (Yvan) of the name John, is used throughout, to avoid possible confusion with some one else who bore the same name.

Which Draws the Portrait of the Youth

Before reaching the highest standard he was already making personal notes, and among these the general trend of his thoughts can be gathered from one brief note, "there is no real virtue without loving *God Alone*." Divine love was, undoubtedly, the elemental foundation in that chosen soul, the secret of his perfect consistency and balance. An old aunt, with one strong stroke portrayed her nephew's psychology: "that child," she said, "exhales the good spirit of God."

Hence it is that a harmonious unity of thought and feeling were remarked in Yvan as a youth: filial piety, friendship, attachment to duty, and admiration for the beauties of nature, all flowed from the same principle. The flame that he bore in his heart, shed its rays on his whole existence. In his eyes, paternal authority bore a priestly character; his parents exercised a vital ministry on his soul, a genial action at once sweet and efficacious, establishing, in the order of Providence, the heredity of virtue. Yvan felt this, unconsciously: he loved the tender shielding of his father and mother and allowed himself to be led by the hand, thus feeling at the same time the dependence and the joy of childhood.

When he left home to complete his course of humanities at Maredsous, the letters he wrote to his father were like a manifestation of conscience to a confessor. He unfolds in them his little weaknesses, his joys and his troubles; he keeps nothing back. "You see, my dearest papa, I have told you about my studies and about my soul—now I am going to tell you how my health is, that you may know *all* about me...." At the end of each letter to his parents he never failed to beg the holy parental Blessing, which is that of God Himself.

On one occasion he writes.

> It is impossible that your Blessing should not bring forth fruit where there is a good will—I feel this every day. Your action on my soul by this means is very strong, and I never neglect to make great use of it.

When he actually left home, to enter upon College life, his father sent him touching recommendations in writing, to the reading of which he attached great value and very special influence. At night, kneeling in his compartment of the dormitory, Yvan read and re-read these precious pages, kissing them respectfully, and seeming to feel again his fathers' hand tracing the Cross on his forehead, as he had so often done in the past.

> "Every evening," he wrote on January 31, 1897, "before going to bed, I think of the blessing and kiss you always gave us at the end of your prayers, and I never forget to read over again the dear good advice you wrote to me; and it seems to me that your Guardian Angel comes—as you said—to bring me my share, which I never cede to anyone else. This is what one cannot do without, no matter what career is followed."

This feeling of religious veneration did not interfere with a warm and tender affection. Yvan loves, he says, his parents "with that devoted filial love that God alone can implant in the heart."

The Sunday letter which all children owe to their parents at the end of the week, was his special delight. "Dearest and best Mama," he writes in one, "for the last two days I have been impatiently looking forward to the delicious time of writing to you"—and he lets his pen run on exuberantly.

There is the same epistolary abundance in his letters to his brothers; and, as one of these was surprised by the length at which Yvan wrote, he replied: "This is how I find the time; I write at every vacant moment—every scrap—and as fast as ever I can! This is how I contrive to have such nice, long chats with you, which I greatly enjoy!"

Family affection was not at all a matter of convention or of routine to him, he lived in and drew nourishment from those incomparable

Which Draws the Portrait of the Youth

consolations that God hides in the home circle and which so few know how to find and value. He appreciated and used the joy (which is worth so many others), of "feeling himself surrounded by hearts capable of loving much and generously."

To his love for his relations, many solid and durable friendships were added, and these were found in a region superior to all merely earthly affection. Thus a young girl writes to him.

> To meet you was a double pleasure during our stay at N. What happy hours we spent! (they were only too short) talking about our good God! Yes, it is indeed true that those who love Jesus easily understand each other.

Yvan's heart echoed to everything that spoke of God, but to one friend in particular his soul vibrated in sympathy, in a home where he could go and spend hours of intimate happiness. After he had left for the cloister a girl friend wrote recalling those happy hours to his memory.

> So our happy little stay at B. is now a thing of the past! we remember that enjoyable time at once with pleasure and regret. That delightful excursion to F. and D.! our return on the river, in the midst of enchanting scenery, whilst, with the stroke of the oars you were cleaving a way through the tumultuous torrent—the amusing scampering over the meadow—the work of making bridges and dykes—the rides on horseback over hill and dale—lastly, and above all else, our confidential chats in the chimney corner—all this was joyous indeed, and will often come back in thought…the blank left by your departure has been great—we seek for you everywhere!

Later on, the monk will come back to his friend, and we shall find him singing the praises of this union which time had but strengthened and made more delightful.

A Benedictine Soul

In his new surroundings Yvan soon knew how to shed joy and to do good. With children he was to be found ever sacrificing himself to please others, without seeming to put himself out at all. He was sure to notice if anyone were left out and to draw him into the game, bringing life and spirit everywhere.

At Maredsous he won the sympathy and esteem of his fellow-students immediately, and by the end of three months he was unanimously named prefect of the Congregation of the Blessed Virgin, and vice-president of the Society of St. Vincent de Paul. This was contrary to all former custom.

Without making any apparent effort, he exercised an excellent influence over his companions, inducing them by his own example to communicate frequently. It was a long time before the Pontifical Decree had appeared, and some people were astonished to see Yvan receive Holy Communion four times every week. The surprise soon wore off, and he could write to his father. "I am not now the only communicant during the week; almost every day someone or other of the students approaches the holy Table, and this is, indeed, consoling. Soon, the Altar rail will be invaded every morning."

Besides all this, Yvan proved that he was capable of close application to study. In this respect, private tuition generally leaves much to the desired. It was so, in Yvan's case; when the young collegian had to face themes and essays without the use of a dictionary, he found himself out of countenance, and wrote thus to his mother.

> Father H.—has just given us a translation to make without dictionary, but as, now, the use of Latin is in abeyance as a medium of general communication, when the dictionary is taken away from us, we lose our "better half." Our professors call this "Modern degeneration."

Which Draws the Portrait of the Youth

He is somewhat sceptical about this term of *degeneration*; but duty lies before him, he will go on toiling and know how to win an honourable place in his class.

"Life," he writes with ingenious conviction—"life is not a game, but a time of preparation for eternal happiness. When I remind myself of this, I start working with renewed ardour. As to the children of 'freethinkers,' it must be difficult to induce them to learn, for the unfortunate little things only obey when they are compelled."

There was one more characteristic note in Yvan's tastes that remains to be mentioned, and that one is his love of nature.

At some distance from his grandfather's home there was a little Chapel, lost in the woods, and called the "Chapel of the heath," from the expanse of heather that lay around it. Every Friday, Mass was said there and Yvan thought it a great treat to assist, starting very early, when the sun had hardly risen, nature was awaking and the air cool and fresh. Along the sandy paths fringed with fir woods, grey rabbits might be seen, frisking their little white tails and scampering away at the least alien noise: the jays and magpies, disturbed in their frolics, made the woods echo with their discordant voices. At last, a little bell tower covered with lichen appeared among the trees, and from thence was heard a cracked, tinkling sound. All around, weirdly shaped oaks raised stunted heads, and in their shadow a few cottages with smoking chimneys nestled. This sylvan sanctuary occupied the centre of a clearing carpeted with crimson heather, and crossed by beaten paths.

How majestic the holy Sacrifice seemed, in such a solitude, and how sweet it was to receive Jesus among these poor wood-cutters!

Yvan was neither dreamy nor melancholy by nature, yet such was the charm this impressive view of nature exercised over him that he was, as it were, transfixed, and wrote from college.

What lovely weather! This morning when at a quarter past seven we went to recreation and breathed the delicious fresh air and looked up at the infinite depths of the sky, I felt I could contemplate these beauties forever! Unfortunately, the pupils are a distraction. You would not believe what I feel when thinking of God in the early morning! It is impossible not to find Him everywhere around one—I fall into such raptures as draw me out of myself!

From all this we draw the inevitable conclusion that Yvan is born to exercise the art of love—the love of God. This comprises every thing to him, and he wrote, later on…

Man is formed and born to love—it is the very reason of his being: his only need is to love, his only joy, his only strength lies in loving. But it is to love Thee, oh! my God, that man exists, the need that urges him is that of Thy love; he becomes strong in loving Thee, the rest he enjoys in Thee is his only true repose and bliss. And so, the heart of man never ceases to seek after Thee until he loses himself in Thee, oh! uncreated Love!

Chapter II

The Vocation

How good it is to have no other end or aim but that of perfect love.

"Letter", December 4, 1897

It was in April 1896, after a pilgrimage to the shrine of our Lady of Hal, that Yvan laid before his parents his desire for the religious life, being then sixteen years old. Let him tell us, himself, in his own way all that happened.

> The other day, being alone with papa and mama, I told them of the keen desire I feel to give myself to God, and once again the goodness of my father was vividly apparent. He replied that he would never put any obstacle in the way of such an excellent project. But, as I asked to be allowed to enter at once, without any University course, he answered that it was yet too soon to decide; that God would arrange things in His own time.

To find the origin of Yvan's vocation, we must seek further than his childhood, nor even stop at the consecration his mother made of her unborn child. For the Source was God alone, whose love has mysterious predilections. The Church says, of holy souls, "elegit eam et pre-elegit eam"—God chose him for Himself.

In his "Thoughts," written later, Dom Pius (as he then was) really unfolds his life-story and ponders over that question of Vocation with dreamy grace.

> "Why," he asks himself, "why should a pure soul withdraw into solitude? Why should that soul, so full of tender sympathies, so well adapted to enjoy the beauties of nature, yet hide itself in an austere cloister?"[7]

This sort of "folly" has, indeed, no other cause than a special design on the part of Providence. Often, the divine predilection manifests itself by a compelling attraction, a secret and persistent impulse towards eternal things; such was Yvan's case. This beautiful vocation had a perfectly decisive character; it had been prepared by a profusion of gifts, natural as well as supernatural, and would seem not to have been hindered by the numberless circumstances which often veil the Finger of God.

Hence it is, that, in Yvan's eyes the Religious Life was really a love affair, a *Call* to union with the Beloved: "Come to the marriage." The letters he wrote during his novitiate show this very clearly. He writes:

> I simply and solely desire this life of union by love. What other wish could a monk have? That he might be able to contemplate our God, and sing His praises unceasingly.

Being thus in love with God alone, Yvan knew to what he was called, the sails of his soul were set for the course he had to take, and he would not waste time in groping to find his way. Neither did he hesitate in the choice of the Order he would enter. The place he

---

[7] "Thoughts."

The Vocation

sought was one "made for love," a monastery, a cloister perfumed with the fragrance of silence and of prayer. His soul had no other ambition than to love God and to live in His holy Will by an entire gift of self to Jesus-Christ. No higher desire could actuate a young heart that was ardent and generous as his was. He could not dream of a nobler ideal of life, and no more was needed to establish a singular affinity between the monastery and himself. A Benedictine Abbey is called a "School for the service of God."[8] It was by His submission to His Father's Will from the "moment of His entrance into the world"[9] until His "consummation" on the Cross, that Christ restored all things and has drawn them back to God. It is also by the "labour of obedience" that the monk who is His disciple even unto death, must return to his Creator. It is by this obedience that he pursues, under the action of the Holy Spirit, his secret search after Christian perfection in its integrity. It is this Obedience, too, that in the life of the monk as in the Life of Christ, commands and regulates the practice of every form of secondary activity.

This principle, simple, and vast as the world, and marking with a character of powerful unity all that it touches, is clearly expounded by St. Benedict, and put the young Yvan in a position to understand and relish the wondrous harmony and fruitful amplitude of the life he was going to embrace. Any other kind of life, dominated by pure activity, seemed to him as an existence wherein the soul, dissipated and dispersed, allows the intensity of its love to relax, and its cohesion with God to weaken.

Yet, notwithstanding all these assurances, Yvan had his share of those struggles, fears and throes which go to make up what may be called the crisis of a vocation. At the critical parting of the ways, when

---

[8] *Prologue* to the Holy Rule of St. Benedict.
[9] Heb.: x, 5.

the time came for the final choice, the soul of the youth was seized with indefinable disquiet; it was the *"tug of war"* between secular love and that which is divine; the fear of being mistaken, after all; disgust at the undecided situation in which, for the time, he found himself, together with uncertainty as to the future.

Finally, it was the necessity of abandoning himself, once for all, to blind *Faith*. He writes from College.

> I am tormented by all sorts of thoughts, and, do what I will, they hardly ever leave me! Papa tells me to say to God, "I am ready, Lord: speak but the word and I will come." Then to turn out all these worrying thoughts and throw them out of the window. In theory I find this excellent, but in practice I don't succeed.

As the time for his entrance into the Order drew near, Yvan's soul became more and more in the grip of these trials. He writes.

> My enthusiastic desire for the great moment is strangely chilled before the hardness of the sacrifice I have to make. Do not think that I am going to change, or alter my decision; but nature is making a great fuss! I have to calm it, or combat it, until I make it hold its tongue—for it brings before my mind all the bodily privations and rigours which add to the moral sacrifice and pain of separation. All this was against the Spirit...the heart does not yet belong entirely to Jesus, and it is troubled and made to suffer. The other day I went to Audenarde with X., and when I saw the Carmelite Convent, I could not help shuddering and felt a kind of horror. But I left that holy house deeply moved at seeing the peace and joy imprinted on dear M's face. At that moment I could willingly have endured all for God—and now,—already—I am frozen up again! Pray for me to our Lady of Sorrows, it is to Her we must have recourse!—let us *implore* her help!—above all, in the present circumstances, our Lady of Dolours.

The Vocation

Up to the very last days, Yvan was tossed about by these disturbances. Sometimes the cloister appeared to him in brilliant colours, and he was carried away by the charms of solitude and the sweetness of divine Love; but at other times it seemed quite the contrary and as if he were entering on an "abominable business"—and then he was half inclined to back out of it.

As we can see, even the most well-founded vocations are liable to such shocks as these, of a violence which shakes the very soul. Before the resolution to live for God alone, the reason remains confounded, as it does in an act of faith. The religious vocation has its own motives of credibility, and, when these are once firmly established, the soul must go on without any faltering.

On December 8th 1897, the Feast of the Immaculate Conception of our Lady, Yvan entered at Maredsous. At the same time one of his brothers went to La Trappe at Chimay. It was a trying day, and Yvan's sensitive nature suffered much from the separation as well as from the grief of his parents who accompanied the two brothers to their respective destinations.

The door of the cloister closed upon him; but the painful impression he had felt for several months now came upon him worse than ever before, and on December 11th he writes:

> Here I am—at last; at Maredsous! I have not yet received the holy habit and I am longing to get it. Just now, it fills me with dismay—yet I am in hot haste to make its closer acquaintance. Whilst waiting, the service of God seems hard and dry.—I don't know what I am, nor what I am doing—and if I did not see the Hand of God in all that, I could not endure such a painful life!… But I should do wrong to complain, for A's courage would put me to shame! That dear, good fellow has entered La Trappe with admirable courage and energy—and he'll need it all, too—to embrace a life of that kind. How beautiful such renunciation is! Let us pray to God for

our good brother, and ask for strength for him—we must pray a lot—and also for our good parents too, who have made a double sacrifice with rare generosity. Poor Mama was so overcome, it made me feel bad to see her! Our good papa kept his feelings under, so that he might go on encouraging us all the time. I do pray God to reward them both *largely*—even here below—for their goodness. Finally, beg God to inflame us both with His love; that is the only thing to be desired. He must consume us entirely.

On the following day (December 12) he wrote to his brother at La Trappe:

I am thinking too much of you to be able to resist my longing to write, so I asked leave to do so, which was granted as you see. Have you the holy habit yet? and how are you? As for myself, I am not yet clothed—I long to be so, for I feel 'all over the place.'[10] How lovely it is to belong to God entirely!… although up to now I have only tasted the bitterness of separation and the dryness of beginning. But, beyond this thorny hedge I can see the fair colours of the garden of roses, and their sweet scent floats over to me. I flounder about in the Breviary energetically, and will say an office for you, when I am more at home with it. I find the Breviary beautiful, and such good food for the soul.…I give you a warm kiss, dearest A., in the depths of my heart, and it seems to me that I love you even better than ever (if that were possible) since we have both been given entirely to God.

The Clothing took place on December 16 and, under the habit and under the shadow of the black hood, Yvan suddenly found again his former habitual calm and joyous liberty of spirit.

---

[10] Literally, 'I feel rather lost' (*je me sens assez perdu*).

The Vocation

"Three words," he wrote to his Abbot, who was then at Rome, "three words will be enough to tell you the state of my soul, *I am happy.*"

Happy! because he sees the way of love opening before him: after the struggles and fears he had had to go through, he is able to give the following testimony.

I can feel in myself something telling me that I have done as I ought. And then I see that one must love, and love much: without love a monk is imperfect.

Two places in the monastery won his heart at the very outset. The first, which he knew well but not yet to its full depth, was the Chapel of the Blessed Sacrament.

"When I have the ineffable happiness of being allowed to spend some time there," he writes, "and when I find myself mute and fascinated before Jesus Who looks at me from the interior of the Tabernacle, I could stay there for hours. It needs an effort of the will to tear myself away!"

After the Tabernacle, his favourite place was his beloved cell.

Peace reigns there—one is alone with God, and in that deep recollection one feels what one really is—the soul is seized with a vehement longing after perfection and complete holy union with God.

It is evident that the little crisis through which Yvan had gone, was an affair of the past; his soul was stedfastly fixed now, and threw itself ardently into its true path for life.

Let us anticipate somewhat, and in future give the young monk the name he received on his entrance into the novitiate: his religious name. Henceforth Yvan would be called Brother Pius, and, as to this he writes to his grandfather.

> I like this beautiful name very much, and feel an interior conviction of the protection of our Lady in the choice of this patron for me. It is She who obtained also the grace of the Vocation; on the Feast of her Immaculate Conception I began my religious life, and now She has confided me to the care of one of her specially faithful children.[11] My holy patron will obtain for me the love of Her by whom we go to Jesus.

---

[11] St. Pius V. was devoted to our Lady: it was during his Pontificate that the Christian armies gained the victory of Lepanto over the Turkish mussulmans owing to the intercession of the Blessed Virgin.

Chapter III

The Novitiate

Father Master introduces us to the mystic death.

Novitiate notes.

The Master of Novices[12] was a monk of great mortification, an old man solely occupied with God, who could not understand how any other pleasure could be sought after in this vale of tears. He was past-master in the art of waging war upon human nature, and, notwithstanding his very real and deep affection for his novices, he was never wanting in his duty of submitting them to the hardest humiliations.

The usual subjects of his Conferences were those of renunciation, abnegation and death to self: he came back upon these, again and again—his "delenda Carthago." This austere teaching was accompanied by a certain brusque, sharp gesture as if he were sweeping aside some invisible obstacle. Nevertheless, his voice, under the special inspiration of grace became thrilling; at certain moments he was evidently

---

[12] Dom Benedict d'Hondt, died at Maredsous in the peace of the Lord December 6, 1908. R.I.P.

moved, his look became illumined, truth flowed from his lips without preparation, without studied phrases, often without definite connection. But the words he spoke were salutary, and sometimes, after a rather dull Conference, at the moment of prayer, unction seemed to overwhelm him.

His conceptions of monasticism recall those of the Fathers of the desert, and were entirely summed up in the grand and simple saying, "conquest of God by the annihilation of self; forgetfulness of the created, to live only in the Infinite." And it was thus that he used to speak in the Conferences in the Noviciate.

Dom Pius himself supplies us with the following notes, remarkable alike for their vigour of thought and their uncompromising tone.

> Everything outside of God is useless and vain; our only End and Aim is God. We are fools indeed if we do not truly and constantly seek God, Who is Joy and Happiness. If we are in the monastery it is only that we may become saints, that we may shake ourselves free from all below, and seek after nothing else but to know our Creator and contemplate Him. He alone *is*; He alone ought to be the Object of our love.…Let us keep our heart free from affection for any created thing. Attachment to any earthly thing is that which is most disturbing—both in the outer world and in our own souls. As soon as we are attached to creatures, we separate ourselves from God.

Father-Master asked for no ecstacies in his novices. Above all, they must, as St. Benedict teaches,[13] learn to Obey; to submit their wills, humbly and cheerfully to their superiors; die to selfwill "the great enemy," and know, as Christ taught, to make themselves little, to become as little children: "Nisi efficiamini sicut parvuli."

---

[13] Prologue, Holy Rule, also ch. V. and ch. LVIII.

The Novitiate

Brother Pius, who had always loved and valued the authority of his parents, now gave himself up to his Father-Master with filial abandonment, becoming closely united to him, and looking to him for guidance in the new life. Thus, he writes to his mother:

> Our Lord wishes to form me by the hands of our good Father-Master; it is he who gives us the sublime life of Christ. To wish to do without him, would be to withdraw ourselves from God.

In practice, he showed this filial spirit by an absolute dependence. St. Benedict reckons "eagerness for obedience" as one of the marks of a true monastic vocation.[14]—"The end a monk must have in view is an unfaltering love for Christ." Obedience is the most excellent of all means for attaining that loving union, owing to the likeness it reproduces between the disciple and the Master. "Who was made Obedient even unto death" and it is this singular efficacy that gives to Obedience its inestimable value in the eyes of a faithful monk, (*Holy Rule c. LXXI*,) who thus (as did our zealous novice) takes pains to attain as far as in him lies, to what S. Benedict calls "Obedientie bonum," the "excellence of Obedience."

Brother Pius was minute in his practice of this great monastic virtue. Never did he write a letter without mentioning humbly that he had leave to do so. Being anxious to submit and to abase himself, he would be everyone's servant, constantly seeking occasions to do a kind act and take the drudgery on himself. If any work had to be shared with others, he always found a way to get the hardest part for himself. When the water ran short in the tanks, he foresaw the needs of the brethren, and pumped away whilst the perspiration ran down his face. In winter, when the novices had to wash the pavement in the church, Brother Pius managed, unostentatiously to get

---

[14] *Prologue*, also ch. V and LVIII.

possession of the wet cloths that had been used, and rinsed them out in ice-cold water, regardless of the chilblains on his hands. His love of obedience led him to carry always about with him a copy of the Holy Rule—that code of perfection left by the Patriarch of monks to his sons and which Brother Pius used to call the "living relic of holy Father Benedict." The first and last pages of this copy are covered with notes and "Thoughts," some in his own hand and some written by his superiors, brothers and friends. There is real warmth in this little "jewel-case," and it gives the impression that here, as everywhere else, he felt the need of *sharing* his love.

Identifying his Rule with his Lord, Brother Pius writes in it these words of his divine Master: "Qui me confessus fuerit, confitebor et ego eum coram Patre meo."[15] And lower down on the page he adds, "there is no soul that can ignore the treasures of piety contained in this Rule, except those who have strayed into the paths of sentimentalism."

All this shows that Brother Pius was faithful to the least of the regular observances and to the most minute customs of the house: the details sometimes seemed to him trivial, perhaps even useless, but he only sought to subdue his own judgment and act contrary to his own caprice.

Being convinced that the smallest habits of curiosity, talkativeness or other lightness lead to relaxation and weaken the interior life of a monk, he made a point of trying to avoid every cause of dissipation, closing his eyes, his ears and his mouth, and retiring into silence. With real constraint he applied himself to being interiorly recollected. At first, he was not so. One day, for example, when Brother Pius was busy in the sacristy, he had an attack of high spirits, and began to pelt his companion with ends of candles. The other was a venerable novice, forty years old, not crabbed, but seeing things in a graver light. He

---

[15] St. Luke, XII, 8.

The Novitiate

made some reflections on his young companion, giving hint what may be called "a piece of his mind" which went home, and that was the last time that "the collegian cropped up." From that moment Brother Pius sought after perfect recollection.

> "Pray much for me," he wrote to one of his companions, "for I want to live a truly contemplative life—and I do feel in myself so little courage for that *perfect abnegation* which is so indispensable to an interior life! Let us retire into the solitude of our cells, and, above all, into that of our hearts. Let us draw ourselves aside and live retired in God—let us love this *depth* of God!"

Such generous renunciation opened the avenues of the novice's soul to grace; but there its work ended. As a matter of fact, it is but little to mortify the body and selfwill; it is not enough to restrict oneself exclusively to the work of destroying the "old man": To do so, is to risk leaving incomplete the work of perfection and even the whole of the Christian life. Christ, who came upon earth to destroy sin by His Death, did not quit the world without bestowing upon it a source of life. "In the work of Redemption," wrote Brother Pius, "death is the beginning of life"; and the monk, even more than the ordinary Christian, must make this Life his own, by raising the soul, "in making his activity expand in fruits of holiness by his union with Christ." Was not this the whole ambition of the young novice? And he was not to be disappointed: he was now going to find the instrument to help powerfully in the ascension of his soul towards God. He found it in the Liturgy.

In the course of the liturgical year, devotion is fed by the contact, ceaselessly renewed, with the sacred formularies gathered together by the Church herself, in the Breviary and the Missal. The soul makes the ardent aspirations of the Psalmist her own, feeds on the marrow of the Gospels and on the strong doctrine of the Fathers. Raised as by a lever, she mounts up naturally towards heaven. By thus following, with the Church the Spouse of Christ, the cycle of the Mysteries of her Lord, she unites herself even to the very Person of the Author of all Grace; she enters into His sentiments and participates in His Sacrifice, as she shares in His merits. In this ceaseless union with the Divine Word, she imbibes the secret of a virtue so much the more solid and fruitful as its Source is the less human and utterly inexhaustible.[16]

---

[16] A Benedictine monk when taking upon himself the obligation of the Divine Office, by this new act possesses—or puts himself in the way of possessing—the "better part." But this he does not keep for himself. He is deputed by the Church to sing the divine praises, he is constituted spokesman for all Christianity (*os totius Ecclesiae*) and must make his voice heard by Christ, who listens to him, as to "the voice of the Bride," and his action, hidden as it may be in the depths of God, resounds through all the earth!

Let us add that it is necessary to understand that the Divine Office is not the exclusive end of the monk's life, for such an idea would be too limited, and a contradiction to the spirit of the Rule. The Order of St. Benedict aims at the complete expansion of Christian life. If a very large place is given to the divine Office "the Work of God" as the holy Founder calls it—this is simply because the praises of God occupy the first rank in all Christian duty. But this does not shut out other means of spreading the knowledge and glory of God and must not be extended so far as to compromise the equilibrium of the Monastic Ideal.

On this title the Benedictine monk in taking on himself the obligation of the divine Office, undoubtedly possesses the "better part." But this he does not keep for himself. Being deputed by the Church to sing the divine praise, and made the mouthpiece of all christians "*os totius Ecclesiae*," he makes his voice sound in the ears of Christ who listens as to the "voice of the Bride," and his action, though hidden as it may be in the depths of God, has its resounding force on all society.

The Order of St. Benedict seeks the full expansion of Christian life. If a very large place is given to the "*Opus Dei*" as the holy Founder calls the Divine Office, it is because in the economy of christianity itself, the praise of God demands this importance. But it is not exclusive and must not be stretched to the point of compromising the equilibrium of the Monastic ideal.

The Novitiate

Brother Pius understood all this. When at College he had been deeply touched by the august spectacle of the ceremonies of the Church without being always able to penetrate the mystery they embody. Now, he chanted the office as a true contemplative, and the psalms and hymns were the spontaneous utterance of the transports of his soul. "It is the heart that sings first," he said: "the song of the lips follows." This was the admirable interpretation he gave to the counsel of the Rule when it recommends "so to sing that the heart and voice may accord together."[17]

In choir, his attitude—all humility and reverence towards God, as St. Benedict desires[18] was very impressive, and a brother monk tells how, one day: "…I remember one day, when my soul was very much disturbed, as I looked at the young brother, who was next to me in the choir, I regained my calmness. His pose, his respect, his devotion moved me to admiration and did me good. Often I tried, without his knowing it, to resemble him, ever so little!"

Understanding the natural connexion that exists between Liturgical and mental prayer, Brother Pius never failed to recollect himself before and after each of the canonical hours, as the ancient monks used to do. He gathered wonderful fruit from these moments of silent prayer which prepared him to offer the divine praise, and afterwards permitted him to enjoy its sweetness.

> The soul sings to God, and then she reposes in Him—she praises the Object of her love and then slumbers in the caress of that Love whom she adores.[19]

Very soon, prayer fed at this ever-burning hearth became his happiness, he devoted all the time at his own disposal to this joy,

---

[17] *Holy Rule*, c. XIX.
[18] *Holy Rule*, c. XX.
[19] "Thoughts," XXXVI.

and took extreme care to acquire and keep up this continual converse with God which gives the soul such great peace. What can the life of a monk be, without this intercourse of the soul with its God? Take from the monk this mystic treasure, and what is left to him? A complete void—inanition—the most devastating anæmia of the heart! Brother Pius felt this keenly, and, with all his characteristic tenacity he pursued his end,—he *would learn* to pray. His Novitiate, though made up of a thousand trifles, will not be trivial, the freedom from worldly concerns in which he lived will not seem empty and fruitless to him; it will allow him to devote himself entirely to the great undertaking.

On November 15, 1898, he writes,

> let us always adore God Who dwells in us. Do not let us be frivolous, for our God, full of wisdom, will not speak unless He knows He will be heard, and we cannot hear Him except in silence and solitude. Let us seek after love; he who possesses that, possesses all, and forever.

He was soon to possess it more completely, for the year of noviciate was drawing to an end: the hour approached when he would make the entire donation of himself, by religious profession.

A few weeks before the longed-for day, Brother Pius received a letter from his father urging him to consider well, and to make his decision with full liberty of spirit. Here is his reply:

> I have asked leave, dear papa, to thank you before Lent for the kindness you have shown me in your last letter. If God willed me to be in the world, I would return unhesitatingly, trusting myself to your fatherly affection. But our good God seems to point out the choice I ought to make, by the happiness He has given me all the time I have been in His House, and by the ardent longing He has put into my heart to consecrate myself to Him alone. My part now is to walk in the path of holiness without sparing myself in any way. By myself, I am quite unable to do this; and

so I beg most earnestly of you to help me by praying and getting prayers for me. Preserve me from unfaithfulness which, as it lessens divine blessings, must lead me to a life of misery: for a tepid monk cannot be a happy one.

As this letter proves, and as, later on, the Father-Master himself assured Dom Pius, his noviciate has passed without any untoward incident and without moral sufferings. For many, this first year of religious life is a period, in the course of which "conversion" is worked out, when the novice alters the direction of his thoughts and of his affections. This change does not take place without interior tortures, disgust, weariness, various troubles from our fallen nature. Dom Pius did not have to endure any of these trying experiences which beginners greatly owe to their particular temperament or to their cowardice. He will suffer, later on; but with the sufferings of the strong.

On March 21, 1899, the Feast of St. Benedict, he was admitted to make his simple vow, together with five of his companions. Before the assembled brethren and the holy relics of the saints kept in the Abbey, he promised "obedience according to the Rule."[20]

To make this oblation of himself more complete and as far as possible one with that of Christ, he placed on the Altar (as St. Benedict enjoins in ch. LVIII of the Rule) during the offertory of the holy Mass, the parchment on which he had written the form of his vows: then, to perfect the symbolism of his immolation, he prostrated during

---

[20] *Rule* of St. Benedict, c. LVIII.—Properly speaking, the Vow of Obedience is the only vow of perfection asked by St. Benedict. For, the "conversion of manners" signifies the life of obedience in its entirety; whilst that of "Stability" an engagement of an essentially administrative order, whatever may be further its importance for the interior life. Or, to put it in a simpler way, "*Conversion of manners*" and "*Stability*" only strengthen the pursuit of perfection, to which the monk obliges himself by his vow of obedience. —According to the Rule (ch. LVIII).

the Canon, under a black pall, remaining thus until the time of the Communion. Then the deacon approached and chanted "Arise from the dead, and Christ will be thy Light." At these words, the newly professed, arising, went to the Altar to receive the Bread which gives life. Henceforward; Dom Pius was a monk. The absolute nature of his promise (which no consecration to a secondary end either strengthens or weakens) establishing him in a state of complete donation to God. From this hour it is lawful for him to pursue under the direction of his Abbot, the end and aim of the monastic life, which is the entire restoration in us of the divine plan, by union with Christ in His Obedience.[21]

The two years which follow *profession*, are dedicated to the study of philosophy, and during the whole of this time the young monks remain under the spiritual direction of the Master of Novices: we shall not pause long over this period, because it does not mark anything special in the interior life of Dom Pius. He worked assiduously, no doubt, but without the power as yet to utilise for his own moral progress, the knowledge he was acquiring. His existence seems at this time divided into two—a partition almost *watertight* separating his interior life from his life of study. Whence came this partition? The young philosopher himself would have been puzzled to answer the question. He was always equally zealous in applying himself to self-annihilation and humiliation, everywhere and in every way: in his letters he writes, with touching unction, of himself as an "unworthy sinner." But his soul was not at ease, and seems to have experienced a false restraint, whilst his progress did not answer to his efforts. In the spiritual atmosphere in which he lived, Brother Pius seemed to feel a want of ease; there was something lacking to him.

---

[21] Prologue to the holy Rule.

The Novitiate

This painful state became more accentuated towards the end of his course of philosophy, but he did not get anxious about it. His docility to superiors never relaxed, nor did his regularity.

"Let us do all things to please God," he wrote, "whatever it may cost us: let us endure these struggles and be on the watch to see the Divine Will. Do not let us be afraid of seeing, but let us be brave enough to correspond by our conduct to the teaching we may meet with—either inward or outward. Let us dispose our souls to receive the light in every place and at any moment; let us strengthen our will and never let it falter. Let us be very faithful, and we shall live."

Indeed, his fidelity and confidence were not to be disappointed. God was preparing his soul for a great flight.

Dom Columba Marmion, Abbot, O.S.B.

Chapter IV

The Years of Study of Theology
The revelation of Love (1900 to 1902).

Grant that I may love Thee, oh Jesus!
there is all my soul's strength.

—From the "Note-book," August 17, 1902

Love, when it is once lighted in the soul, provided
it be kept carefully and delicately tended, is a
spark which grows little by little, and gradually
consumes all that is in the way of its activity.

—"Thoughts," VII

In September, 1900, Dom Columba Marmion, at that time, Prior of the monastery of Louvain preached the annual Retreat at Maredsous.[22]

---

[22] Dom Marmion was already in possession of his Pauline doctrine: the spiritual conferences which he gave from this time form as it were the kernel of the

The strong and inspiring doctrine of the preacher was chiefly directed to making known our Lord Jesus-Christ in the intimate depths of the soul and to establishing a real contact of faith and love between the Shepherd and His sheep. The soul "given up to Christ" is on the road, and walks with cheerful swiftness in the steps of its Master.

This teaching, inspired by St. Francis de Sales, found its first sources in the Epistles of St. Paul and the Rule of St. Benedict.[23] From the heart and lips of Dom Marmion it flowed with vigour and originality.

The light for which Dom Pius had been waiting, was now to shine before his eyes; a new way was to open before him. Full of joy and confidence he went to throw himself at the feet of the preacher of the Retreat; and he writes:

> I gave myself up entirely into the hands of my good Father, and begged him to gain for me that divine Love which alone can fill our souls.

He felt himself in the presence of one who was to be his true father in the order of grace; before long he was to find Dom Marmion at Louvain, where the young monk was to study theology under his direction.

When penetrating the heart which came to give itself up to his guidance, Dom Columba could not restrain a cry of admiration, "to know this dear child better, is to love him more. Divine Wisdom dwells in his pure soul. His prudence astonishes me and his sweet affection delights me!"

---

chapters since published (but not until twenty years later) under the title of "*Christ the Life of the Monk.*"

[23] Notably in the *Prologue*, where it is amply set forth by St. Benedict. On the spiritual relationship between St. Benedict and St. Francis de Sales, see the suggestive pages by Dom Ryelandt in his "Essay on the moral physionomy of St. Benedict" (Paris, 1924).

The Years of Study of Theology

From that moment Dom Pius was, as it were, taken captive by grace, and drawn into a course beyond all human prudence—the "*folly of the Cross,*" until he should be completely spent—even until death—until his loving desire should be satisfied by the beatific and divine union. God seemed to make him aware that, for him, *time* would be short, and that he must attain to the Infinite End in a few years. He confided to a brother, that he was "strongly impressed that he must lose no time," and wrote to his Mother that he "had received a fresh impulse towards our good and sweet Jesus, and that now, more than ever, he longed to serve his Divine Master solely."

Immediately after the retreat, indeed, on the very next day (September 24, 1900) he wrote the first lines in "God's Note-book"—that "*schedule of his heart*" that overflow of his soul, in which he pours out the super abundance of the grace showered lavishly on him. Five times, in the course of September and October, he took up his "Note-book," and wrote therein several pages which are really the germ of the wonderful growth, blossom and fruit, which we are about to study.

With all the energy of his soul, yet with extreme distrust of his own weakness, he makes the irrevocable resolution "*to be faithful to Grace.*" Convinced as he was (from having often read his Rule)[24] of the impotence of man and the Almightiness of God, he grasped the necessity of following the divine Will, step by step, and made up his mind to be docile, humble and obedient, forming the habit of responding fully, exactly and at once to the voice of divine Love.

"Oh! Jesus," he writes, "I abandon myself into Thine Arms, as to the direction of the Holy Spirit. Make of me—do with me—whatever Thou willest, either by Thine own action, or through my superiors or by my brethren and I will try *to obey*

---

[24] *Prologue*, ch. IV, and many other passages.

perfectly. I will do all, oh! Love, in order to put no hindrance to Thine action."

Love! yes: love was the lever of life; the only means of growth! As long as the soul is not *in love* with God, and until she fixes her eyes on the Eternal Beauty alone, she remains frozen, unable to move. In order to live, to grow, to expand—the soul must love!

On October 2, Dom Pius wrote:

Oh! my God, and my only Good! my heart is full of joy—for Thou hast made me understand that all is love—and that, outside of love there is naught. Yes, Jesus! my soul understands this practically, and henceforward it will live no more but by love.... To put myself more completely under the direction of the Holy Spirit, I wish for nothing else but to love in all things and everywhere.

On October 12, 1900, Brother Pius started, together with several of his young brethren, for the Abbey of Mont César at Louvain, where he was to pass four years in studying theology. Situated on a historic hill, formerly crowned by an imperial castle, the monastery dominates the University city whose noise and turmoil surges to the foot of the mount. Twenty theological students led there a regular and peaceful life of study and prayer. Their existence was uniform, but not at all monotonous, for "souls are ever on the move towards growth in love."

Dom Marmion had the double charge of the course of dogma and the spiritual formation of the young monks. He knew by experience that the half light of a dim and grey atmosphere depresses souls, and benumbs them. He wished them to have light, full, abundant, radiant as sunrise. And the professor of dogma possessed a rare quality; he had the gift of making revealed truths to be relished, and of drawing mystical conclusions from them. At the close of his lessons, his pupils were irresistibly drawn to kneel before the Tabernacle, or to recollect themselves in silence in their cells. Thus, theology was a preparation for contemplation; and the students felt that they did not truly know the subjects until they had been thoroughly digested in prayer. As Brother Pius once wrote, "we have finished the Treatise on the Blessed Trinity, *but I do not know it yet by heart."* The "Letters" which will follow later on, will show us the profound effect which the study of the dogmas of the Holy Trinity and of the Incarnation had upon the interior life of the young monk.

In this course, the intellectual orientation of Brother Pius was clearly determined and his mind established itself in the sphere of asceticism. Wide open as that mind was to a crowd of things, it led all to converge upon the science of the saints; the problem which attracted him and around which he applied all the forces of reflection, was that of the moral perfecting of man. Outside of and beyond that preoccupation he considers "theology itself is but a very *parching* metaphysical science."

At the age of twenty-two Dom Pius was possessed of a ripe doctrine, whose character was well defined. On looking through his notes and correspondence it is easy to distinguish the leading thoughts on which he fed. The time had come to secure them, for they were to remain the guide of the rest of his existence.

Benedictine asceticism does not tend to give a "bent"; it simply aims at opening the eyes; it does not present a formula, but principles of life. Instead of tracing an exactly defined programme, it merely points out a general direction. Each saint formed by this system creates a type of sanctity which he does not transmit. Thus, Benedictine asceticism in no way "breaks in" the soul, but rather calls for a flight that can be born of nothing else but the breath of contemplation; it does not draw the soul to a laborious study of itself, but promises perfection by the very development of its faculties—we would rather say, by the total abandonment and complete forgetfulness of *self*, in the thought of the divine Love. The whole work of monastic education is to inculcate the understanding of the fact that the life of the Blessed Trinity is communicated by Christ, in Obedience:[25] these few words are a light—*the* Light that Christ brought into the world (St. John. I. v. 18) and which acts within us as a principle of life. These few words, (it sometimes needs years of the work of divine grace to bring ourselves to pronounce them in our spiritual life) contain in short, three great principles as simple as they are fruitful.

1. God is Love. The love our heavenly Father has for us is the first cause of our sanctification: everything between the soul and God is a question of love.
2. The Second Person of the Blessed Trinity, Jesus-Christ, was made Flesh in order to spread fire on the earth, to give the Holy Spirit. He, the Word Incarnate is the necessary Sacrament of the Mystic Alliance.

Brother Pius wrote, on January 3, 1902:

---

[25] But, someone may ask, what is this? Do you compress in these few words the whole ascetic "manual" of the monk? Yes—undoubtedly —and, better still.

This doctrine is the essence of the incomparable *Prologue* to the Holy Rule and may be briefly reduced to the following points.

1) To attend to the divine Call, and follow its attractions to the Angelic life.
2) To take courageously the Armour of Christ; thus.
3) To undertake the discipline of Obedience unhesitatingly: "To thee, therefore, my words are now addressed, whoever Thou art that, renouncing thine own will, dost put on the strong and bright armour of obedience, in order to fight for Christ the true King... that the labour of obedience may lead thee (to thy Creator). What can be sweeter, Brothers, than this voice of the Lord inviting us?... Who is the man who will have life? Behold, in His Goodness the Lord shows thee the way of life...and, as we go forward in our life and in faith we shall with hearts enlarged and unspeakable sweetness of love run the way of God's Commandments."

The Years of Study of Theology

These last few days, I have understood more clearly that Jesus is for us ALL IN ALL. The desire of possessing Him is the only prayer that ought to be found in the soul, because from this one all others naturally flow, just as all heavenly blessings come from Jesus Himself.

In all Brother Pius' writings there is no other truth that is expressed more forcibly or in a more touching manner than this one.

3. All the powers of the soul, in the presence of Jesus-Christ and of the Holy Spirit, ought to be directed to avoid hampering or paralysing the energies of grace, but to correspond with them actively and faithfully: Brother Pius himself will speak to us of the infinite delicacy of this adaptation of man to the divine action: he will tell us of the care with which the "divine spark kindled in the soul," must be cherished.[26]

At the same time that he is flooded with light, Brother Pius sings aloud the need of love:

The real reason for the being of man, his sole need, his only strength, is *love*[27]....A nature without love is a spring without sunshine[28]....Jesus decided for me that He would never give me anything else to do but to love.[29] The soul of a true monk is a bird that demands the pure, wide blue heavens...and is ravished with joy in the supreme heights where earth is lost to view.[30]

---

[26] In all that he says on this subject, Dom Pius was but the echo—and a very faithful one, too—of the ascetic teaching of his master, Dom Marmion. In his principles it is easy to trace the leading thoughts in the work "Christ the Life of the soul."
[27] "Thoughts," XX.
[28] "Thoughts," XXX.
[29] *Letter, January 7,* 1902.
[30] "Thoughts," XCVIII.

But the soul of Brother Pius thrills under the Hand of God, who possesses, stimulates and sustains him: he is under the stress of a mysterious and powerful action: God dwells within him. Closing his eyes to exterior things, his sight in the interior of his being is strong and full of faith; there he enjoys a vision surpassing the wonders of nature,—and he cries out.

> It is Thyself, oh! Infinite Beauty! that my soul contemplates! It is Thou, oh! devouring Love! Who attracts and holds it prisoner by the bonds of an incomparable Charity.[31]

Plunged into silence, in the recollection of abandonment, he holds converse with Christ, with the Blessed Trinity, with the Blessed Virgin. These are the habitual guests in the sanctuary of his soul,—that "exquisite little sanctuary," where he leads a life that is intense,—that is utterly hidden.

"God's Note-book" contains some fragments of these celestical colloquies, pale reflections of an ideal love which the words of our human language chill and distort.

In the course of the year 1901, Brother Pius, "desiring to multiply his bonds with heaven," made three solemn consecrations of himself. Of these, the first and third were to the Incarnate Word: the second, to the Blessed Virgin. In Brother Pius' eyes a consecration was an act of the greatest consequence, a matter of vital importance; and it was only after long months of consideration and submitting the persistent inspiration of grace to the judgement of Dom Marmion his spiritual Father, that he decided to make the Act.

The first of these was made on March 25th 1901— the Feast of the Communication. Grace had inspired him to take this step and had impelled him interiorly for no less than six months. During the

---

[31] "Thoughts," XVI.

The Years of Study of Theology

September Retreat, the friendship of Christ had appealed to him as the supreme good of the soul: he had no other thought than to give himself up to Jesus with that utter abandonment that makes saints. Inspired by the mystery of the virginal Conception, the spiritual realisation of which his soul demanded, he wrote as follows:

> In the Name of the Most Holy and Indivisible Trinity, on this day of the Feast of the Annunciation to the Blessed Virgin Mary, March 25, 1901.
>
> I, Brother Pius, having heard the voice of the Angel announcing the Incarnation of the Word, knowing that God wishes to renew that mystery in each soul, I though an unworthy sinner, wish to receive this Messenger with the Blessed Virgin, and with Her to say to him 'behold the handmaid of the Lord, be it done to me according to thy word.' By this I mean to unite myself to the Blessed Virgin, to give myself up, body and soul to the divine Word; in order that, dead to the world by the monastic vows, I may grow unceasingly, under the action of the Holy Ghost, in Christ who is our Head.
>
> I do this for the glory of the Church triumphant, for the welfare of the Church militant; for the relief of the Church suffering.
>
> I do it in the presence of the Father that He may overshadow me with His Almighty power: in the presence of the Holy Ghost that He may come down within me. May the Blessed Virgin Mary, St. John and our holy Father St. Benedict, all the Saints and my beloved Father who authorises me to make this act, all be witnesses of this engagement.

The fruits of this consecration were abundant and the divine Saviour manifested Himself generously to the soul of the young monk, who became, as one of his companions said, "the *mad lover* of Jesus."

Everywhere, the thought of the Master followed him, he felt the invisible Presence at his side, of the Holy One who shared his life.

Long hours, passed at the foot of the Tabernacle, fled like moments in the stillness of divine recollection. "How many things our Master says to me in His silence"; he wrote; "*there*, indeed, is a golden silence."

On Christmas Day, a fresh consecration confirmed and crowned that of March 25, and it is worthy of remark that this union with Christ could not take place without a similar grace in connexion with the Blessed Virgin.

On June 23, 1901, Brother Pius was the object of a favour of which he writes in the following terms, in a letter of July 21.

> I had made up my mind not to write this to you and to wait until I could speak of it; but patience fails me. You must supply for the brevity of a letter always too short when treating of what passes in the soul. I cannot keep hidden from you any longer, an important grace that Jesus granted me, scarcely a month ago. He has joined my heart to That of His dear Mother Mary and I can live always with Her, as with Jesus; without beads, without anything else but love. It is impossible to think of Jesus without thinking of Mary: one unites oneself to Jesus in order to love Her, and takes refuge in Her heart to abandon oneself to Jesus in the infinite fullness of love which She had for Him.
>
> This is so great a grace that I cannot unfold to you all its effects, by writing. These few words will be enough to beg you to thank God together with me.

Such is the divine order of things: to come to the Father, we must do so by Jesus; to come to Jesus, we must do so by Mary.

"God's Note-book" enables us to lay our finger upon the reason and the necessity for devotion to the Blessed Virgin. Addressing the Mother of Christ, he says:

> It is thou who first taught me to walk in the path of close union with thy divine Son, and it is to Him, hidden in thy Bosom that I have consecrated myself this year, for thou dost understand

The Years of Study of Theology

how I cannot come near to thine Only Son, without feeling myself in thy tender Heart. And indeed, thou alone knowest the recollection and care I must have in order to develop Him in my soul, as thou didst when bearing Him within thyself. With thee, then, I desire to live, for I feel only one need, and that one is to belong to Jesus so that I belong to the Father. I bind myself to go to Jesus only by *thee*.[32]

During his noviciate, Brother Pius had said the Rosary wearily: now, he entered into the intimacy of privileged souls, and writes:

> This most Blessed Virgin seems to me so radiant, so full of mercy and tenderness that the thought only of Her, is enough to ravish my soul and fill it with lively Joy.

His filial love suggests a thousand ways of showing it outwardly, with almost infantile affection. Before he slept, he would kiss her scapular and say, "when at night I kiss thy scapular, thou knowest, oh! beloved Mother—the kiss is for thee." He never failed to wear the rosary of the Seven Dolours, for his heart melted and softened at the thought of her sufferings.

Brother Pius consecrated his cell to Mary, and, far more, the sanctuary of his heart and soul, "those holy solitudes, where I would unite myself to Jesus, under the eyes of His Mother."

This flow of graces in so marked a direction, called for a formal response from Brother Pius, and he notes the 15th of August by an act of donation.

> My soul—vowed as it has been to the Divine Word by a perpetual and solemn contract—now desires to enter into a deeper solitude where it may be devoted to prayer and give full vent to its love of my sweetest Spouse. My heart intends to retire into

---

[32] "God's Note-book," June, 22, 1905.

itself by more perfect recollection. Therefore, making a sacred shrine of my miserable little heart, I humbly entreat our Lord Jesus-Christ to come Himself and consecrate that unworthy sanctuary to the honour of Her who is His holy Mother and mine, whose glorious Assumption we celebrate today.

Oh! beloved Mother, I am thine forever! Thou wilt come down into my heart, and I will enter into thine, where I know I can never fail to have mercy from Thy divine Son. Accept, I pray thee, the poor dwelling of my heart, which, for love of thy sweetest Jesus, thou wilt adorn with thy presence. There shall I contemplate Him, and be transformed into His Likeness; and the Spirit of the Lord will raise me up, until, by the Hands of the Son and of the Mother I shall be led from glory unto glory, until I am wholly, entirely to the glory of God the Father.

To attentive eyes these particular graces mark the Sovereign power of the divine action, and are often to be met with in the lives of holy mystics: they were not the only ones which signalised the year 1901.

In proportion as Brother Pius united himself more closely to Christ, so his love for souls grew purer and greater.

Our Well-Beloved has enlightened me much these last few days," he writes in October 1901, "and has spoken eloquently to me of charity. Up to this time I had been satisfied, in a way, with the first part of the precept and had penetrated very little into the second, the new commandment: *Mandatum novum*. One thing I now see clearly, which is, that in the interior life the soul cannot withdraw from the outer world that surrounds it, to love only Christ, hidden in itself....We ought to unite ourselves together in one only love, which must be so intense as to banish egotism from amongst us, as from the Persons of the Blessed Trinity.

Properly speaking, the members of a Benedictine Community constitute a family under the paternal authority of the Abbot, who

The Years of Study of Theology

represents Christ.[33] The conventual life, when led consistently with this principle, serves for nothing less than to draw together souls who are all animated by one and the same desire of perfection. And thus, when a monastery is really fervent, when all the souls there are drawing their nourishment from the fountain of prayer and are filled with God, a sweet bond of fraternity exists between all, which is at once the reason for and the precious treasure of the coenobitical life. These souls understand each other without need of words; for they vibrate in unison in the perfect concord of a common love, having all but one aspiration, one inexplicable yearning—that of possessing God, and of seeking Him alone.

Brother Pius understood this in a wonderful way: and he gave himself unreservedly to his monastic family. He showed that consideration and forbearance in his dealings with his brethren which are the delight of a united family; he was never exacting or self-assertive. In order to act with "the good zeal for others, that monks ought to have"[34] he considered beforehand with the refinement of charity, how to do those little kindnesses which sometimes leave such lasting memories in the souls of those who receive them.

But his loving and open nature asked more than this: it sought for intimacy.

> "Jesus-Christ," he said, "is on intimate terms with every soul that loves Him: and all of them share in this privilege according to the degree of their union with Him."

He longed to see among all men a communicative friendliness, with reciprocal kindly relations dictated by the heart and the soul, where the tenderest and holiest of affections take birth. The Christ Whom he bore

---

[33] *Rule*, c. II.
[34] *Rule*, ch. LXXII.

within him—that joy and peace, those movements of grace to which he was so sensible—ought, in his opinion, to be the natural subject of the monks' conversation among themselves: and, indeed, he knew how to awake echoes from Souls that seemed stricken with dumbness!

These confidences generally took place during the regular walks which formed part of the monastic recreations. The bell rang punctually at the hour for these, and, shod with thick boots studded with nails, after a short prayer everyone set out—two and two, or three or four together, according as inclination led them. Brother Pius would be among them. At first the talk ran on things of small importance, but gradually it would take a higher tone and turn upon theology, rising to God and spirituality. Then Brother Pius could give free vent to the thoughts of which his mind was always full and he spoke volubly, with a simplicity and penetration of which his writings give us some idea. He became the centre of a sympathetic group, for in his whole manner there was something radiant, a sort of halo of grace shone around him. He was aware of this, and took fright at it, lest he might attract and admit any other love than that of God alone. And so he prays, and writes:

> Oh! great God! if it should happen that I please men—look into the depths of my soul and see my firm determination to aim at pleasing Thee alone. That I may do so and never fail, is the grace I now implore from Thy mercy.[35]

The expansive charity of Brother Pius always kept its ideal freshness, and, if more reserve and experience came with age, no poisonous misanthropy or distrust ever dimmed his heart.

His superiors were quick to observe and use this facility of entering into communication with other souls and of exciting in them the

---

[35] "Thoughts," LVII.

The Years of Study of Theology

flames of divine love. More than once, notwithstanding his youth he was chosen to settle and strengthen those who were wavering; and no one can measure the zeal and devotion with which he gave himself to his brethren; it was, indeed, without limit. Even at seasons of greatest pressure such as the heat of theological examinations, he never lacked time when it was a question of the souls confided to him, nor did he ever fail to give kind words and encouragement. With the fervour of his age and the convictions of his deep piety he took upon himself the trials of his brothers, and mingled his tears with theirs. Brother Pius exercised this ministry of charity for three years, and God only knows what a source of merit it was for him. The Cross weighed heavily on him sometimes, but, as he tells us himself in his "Thoughts":[36]

> It is only by suffering that one can save souls; by letting oneself be used up, and, so to say, eaten up alive by the famished souls who have recourse to us. Jesus-Christ, the great Master of souls, has given His flesh for their Food and spared no part of Himself. And no one who receives the charge of souls is free of the duty of nourishing them at all costs to self.

Although not yet a priest, Brother Pius had the mature sacerdotal spirit, and knew the pains and griefs of travailing for souls. His zeal embraced the Church, and all the needs of humanity: for the holy souls in purgatory he made the heroic act, and, in each of the Communions of which we have already spoken, he renewed the offering of his life for the triumph of the Church, the beloved Spouse of Christ.

Two characterising marks of divine love were at this epoch noticeable in the life of the young monk, and each gives a proof of its solidity: its efficacious drawing of his soul, and its extreme refinement. He tells us himself that he had two chief defects, "an excessive need

---

[36] ch. LXXXV.

of pouring himself out, and a foolish way of laying down the law about everything." It can easily be understood. His heart overflowed with love—how could he hold it back?—and the zeal that animated his soul could hardly be kept in. However, living as he did on a high plane, he often saw things in a grandiose manner and overlooked the confused mass of details, so that he gave out judgments which, to him, seemed to admit of no appeal, but which shocked the independence of certain minds. The assurance of his tone might appear to be self-sufficiency, but it was generally the result of his clear-sightedness. Mistakes in this connection were easy; he, himself, was the first to doubt—and in many passages of his "Thoughts" he searchingly analyses this weakness of his:

> A nature that is absolute in its ideas and sympathies, is inaccessible to others....Pride of mind believes that it knows everything, and does not even perceive the fog of ignorance which really clouds every part of it: it shuts itself up in itself, and from that stronghold judges and dominates all that approaches it: full of disdainful assurance it lifts up its voice and speaks with conviction and certitude. These uncompromising natures are lacking in sweetness and affability; they are brusque, hasty and unruly.[37]

Whilst Brother Pius exaggerated his own failings on this point, he saw clearly that it was so contrary to the spirit of Christ that he must take pains to overcome them. "It needs very serious efforts," he writes, "to root out these faults, for they are deeply rooted in my evil nature,"[38] and he also ardently desired "to treat everyone with the same love and consideration I would use in serving Jesus Himself." The "very serious efforts" did not frighten his generous nature, and

---

[37] From "Thoughts," LIV, LV, LVII, LVIII, LXXIL.
[38] "God's Note-book," July 26, 1902.

The Years of Study of Theology

he applied himself to realize his desires with such success that soon Dom Marmion could say, jokingly, to Brother Pius' mother, "Your son was born with the Tiara—now he only wears the mitre!" This was still too much. He learnt how to get rid of it.

Many little experiences combined to teach Brother Pius that though God is not "fussily minute," His action is infinitely delicate. In December, 1900, he was present at the religious profession of one of his brothers in the Order of St. Francis. On this occasion he went home for a little while, and tasted all the sweetness of affection that surrounded him there.

> "For all that," he wrote, "I never ceased to throw myself into the Heart of our Beloved, telling Him that I was only there by obedience and for love of Him. But, notwithstanding, when the moment came for me to leave, I felt my heart *ache*, because for me it was once again like breaking off family life when I had hardly rejoined it. I do not know if this was wrong, but certainly I did not feel Jesus so *intimately* dwelling in my heart as before. During the journey back, I found Him again within me and loved Him, assuring Him that this tenderness of my heart belonged to Him alone. But, even so, I was not able to see Him with the same peace of soul as when I left to go home. I do not complain of Him, for this dear Saviour has led me from here; but I think I have taken too much pleasure in those whom I ought to love only in Him."

And it is so—giving way to affection that is too natural will brush the bloom off the divine intimacy; as Brother Pius himself said in his "Thoughts"[39]: "The apprenticeship of love demands from the soul constant attention to the pursuit of its Good."

---

[39] "Thoughts," XXXII.

A Benedictine Soul

The greater part of Brother Pius' notes dates from this period of his life; we shall send the reader to seek in them the completion of this rapid sketch. These years had seen the dawning of many graces; they were truly "the time of flowers"—fragrant, fresh and fair, but neither the most useful nor the most fecund. A laborious time naturally follows: the burning heat of the summer sun, that will bring the fruit to maturity.

Chapter V

He Studies Theology

The meeting with suffering (1902-1904)

> *The life of a holy soul flows towards suffering as naturally as the river runs to the sea.*
>
> —"Thoughts," LXXIV

Brother Pius was now twenty-two years old. Ever since his infancy the spark of divine Love had been gradually developing within him and had now become a burning and shining flame. This ascent had not been effected without persevering effort nor without great expenditure of energy: but Brother Pius had not yet met with suffering. Now the day had dawned when it would be shed over his soul "like a burning liquid poured over an open sore."[40]

It is often to be remarked, in the lives of great souls, that these come a mysterious "crossing of the ways," where love, after having disengaged them from the world and from themselves, becomes their cruel and blessed martyrdom. "Their thirst for love is to them

---

[40] "Thoughts," XC.

an incessant suffering."[41] Brother Pius experienced this. He felt himself torn to pieces by the Infinite Good, which, at one and the same time attracted him with an irresistible force, and hid itself in the clouds of Faith. "Oh! my God," he cries out, "Thou hast given me a heart of fire which tortures me ceaselessly, either by the excess of its longings for Thee or by the privation of Thy Presence."[42] The nearer he drew to the Object of his desires, the more ardently and painfully did they increase within him. His whole strength lay in what he calls the "very simple contact with God"—and yet, as he wrote to his father:

> "Nothing is so painful as to experience the divine action within the soul. It is true," he adds, "this pain is very good and often joyful suffering. I say—often—for I believe that our Good God at times plunges souls into an abyss of suffering, when all joy leaves them, to the end that they may emerge entirely purified. I do not know what He has in reserve for me in the future, nevertheless I pray Him to make me attain to true love—by however hard a road I may be led there."

This change in Brother Pius' soul was not effected all at once. His growth bore always the same character of regularity and harmonious progression that suited his well-balanced nature. In any case we may consider his solemn Profession on March 21, 1902, as the date when the age of suffering began, which continued during all the remainder of his life. It was strongly impressed upon Brother Pius towards that time, that the way he had travelled was as nothing, compared with that which remained for him to go; and that when upon the higher plane, man no longer walks, but is borne along by God; his own work

---

[41] "Thoughts," CXIII.
[42] "Note-book," May 10, 1904.

seems to have come to an end, he has sacrificed everything, "and, still, he feels as if he does not yet love at all."

Thus, he writes in his "Thoughts."[43]

> When a soul has given its all to Thee, oh! my God, and seeks in vain to find anything further that it can offer, when Thy divine Love has thawed away the ice of egotism, and chased coldness from the heart, when we think we have done all, or, at least, that we have neglected nothing in order to gain Thy holy love: and fancy that we love Thee much—then—only then is it given us to see that we are but just beginning to love.

Gathering together all his energies, Brother Pius wished now, by a supreme renunciation, to consecrate all that he had done until that time, and prepare himself for the last work of grace. The occasion for this was furnished by his solemn Profession. Confirming the simple vows which he had made three years before, and rendering them irrevocable, he consolidated the donation of himself to God, and drew closer the bonds which united him with the divine Love. But Brother Pius, nevertheless, considered that all this fell short of what he would fain do for his Beloved: he wished to despoil himself still more of himself.

To the formula of his vows he joined an act which, notwithstanding its length we will give in its entirety. The echoes of this act resounded and were prolonged, as we shall see, even to his death-bed.

> Most holy Trinity—worthy of all love—today Thou hast condescended to cast a glance of infinite mercy on my unworthy little soul in calling it to Thee, and receiving it in a solemn manner, disregarding its weakness and miseries; but, clothed with the merits of Jesus Christ, and strengthened in Him by divine grace, it would respond to Thy Call in all the fullness of love. And, in

---

[43] "Thoughts," XXXVII.

making this solemn Act I intend to renounce the world and all its works, and to do so anew and forever. Beyond this, I renounce *all right to possess* or *to enjoy* anything whatsoever, outside of and beyond Thyself and Thy holy Will. In particular, my only and sweetest Master I give up, for Thy love, my beloved parents, my dear brothers and cherished little sisters, together with my whole family. I abandon all the affection and every kind of good that I might legitimately possess, so that Thou alone mayst be my Treasure. I devote to Thee my body and all its powers, so that it may become one of Thy sweet dwelling places, and that it may bear and endure all the sufferings Thou mayst wish it to bear for souls: I abandon to Thee my soul and all its faculties in order that it may live no longer but by Thy Life. I offer to Thee all my satisfactory works for the solace of the suffering souls—all my prayers and good works. In one word, I give up to Thee my life and all that it includes, so that Thou, oh! beloved Jesus, mayst dispose of it all....

Now, oh! my Lord and my Master, I possess nothing. If I had anything more, I would give it to Thee; still—Thou art mine Thyself! and I give Thee to Thyself my beloved Jesus. The right to dispose of my blood belongs to Thee, but I beg leave to use it in writing this Act, to witness to Thee and promise Thee, that, notwithstanding my extreme weakness and misery, but armed with Thy strength, I implore and expect from Thy merciful goodness that I shall remain faithful to these promises until my blood shall cease to flow in my veins. And all this, my good Master, I intend to renew every time that I shall say to Thee, "Quae placita sunt tibi faciam semper."[44] I beg also the help of my most dear Mother Mary, of St. Benedict on whose Feast I write these lines, to the glory of the most august Trinity and for love of my Blessed Saviour, according to the permission I have received to make this Act.

March 21, 1902

---

[44] St. John, VIII, 29.

He Studies Theology

From this time Dom Pius' life underwent a great change. To the outside beholders nothing seemed different: there was the same recollection, the same charity, the same regularity at the divine Office and daily work. But if we consult his confidential letters and private notes, we easily perceive signs of the spiritual evolution mentioned above. Dom Pius was entering into God's solitude with great strides. He exulted and suffered.

> When love penetrates into the generous soul, it asks for *everything*—one demand follows another until the soul is entirely denuded. Then it feels its own helplessness, but begins to feel it is strong in God.[45]

Let us briefly consider some marks of this interior life, at once so simple and so complex.

As Brother Pius' soul drew nearer to God, to live in His light, he perceived the true proportions of things better than he had done before. The "littleness of the soul is a truth which, henceforward, it sees in God's light—a divine truth, divinely understood." For the first time,

> the soul sees itself in God. The divine Goodness makes its own misery more prominent—the sight of the Infinite teaches it the nothingness of the finite: the heat of the flame of charity makes it feel the coldness that benumbs it—the vision of the ALL produces the understanding and scorn of the NOTHING.[46]

To this keen sense of the nothingness of the creature is now gradually added the feeling of its own moral impurity.

---

[45] "Thoughts," LXXXI.
[46] "Thoughts," LXIX.

"The utter misery of my sinful soul overwhelms and covers me with confusion," he writes to one of his comrades, "do ask our Lord to forgive the daily faults I commit notwithstanding His boundless goodness to me—far from developing and growing as I ought to do, I am only a little sickly, stunted plant—a green-fly—only fit to be cast away with contempt!"

From this time he intensely felt the need of keeping his eyes cast down, and taking the lowest place among his brethren.[47]

Yet another of the effects of divine love is to plunge the soul into solitude—a solitude that, to nature, is terrifying. This is far removed from that which many young people suffer from (and spoilt children most of all), after some months of noviciate. The soul that has come to a sufficient degree of strength, flying alone above earthly things, and being united to God by only the austere bond of arid faith, is suspended in the void.

Brother Pius, notwithstanding all the affection with which he was surrounded, felt himself to be alone. He could find no consolation but in Jesus, and Jesus had wounded his soul and left him to languish. He felt, more than ever, the extreme need of unburdening his soul, and he was dumb. Thus reduced to silence he felt himself worn out and exhausted by a cruel longing. His "Note-book" tells us something of what he was feeling.

> When? when? oh! my Jesus, will that happy day dawn on my soul—that blessed day so often called for—when Thou wilt manifest Thyself to it, and take possession of a heart that belongs to Thee alone?…I cannot think the longed for day can be far off now—for my heart's desires are such that I feel it is drawing near. Even so, the waiting time is long, my beloved, merciful Saviour!

---

[47] See "God's Note-book," March 10, 1904, and also the Rule of S. Benedict, ch. VII.

He Studies Theology

I know that, from the moment when Thou wilt invade my heart, its tortures will increase, Thy love will make it suffer mercilessly. I know the intensity of this divine suffering, nevertheless, I tend towards it with all the energy of my soul.[48]

It was thus that Brother Pius learned to live to God alone, by Him detached from all else; in a solitude such as to make nature say, "the love of God is bitterly cold."

And, to all these bitternesses were added temptations and troubles which cast him down to the depths—the waves and storms swept over his soul: "the day is dark; no star rises to show the way of salvation. My soul is overwhelmed by innumerable passions whose waves carry it away on their mountainous crests to cast it afterwards into the most frightful abysses, and only sweep away to return a hundred times, each with a new and fiercer attack to thrust it down again. Within myself I seem scarcely to find an atom of will to dominate and keep within the limits of God's law."[49]

Still, throughout all, and notwithstanding all, the longing after God continually increased within him. Worldly minds think that suffering poisons the life of pure souls; but, on the contrary, it is a necessary condition of their growth, an essential element in their vocation. Brother Pius was happy in having left the ways of the world, "to run in the paths of Gods love."[50]

Each year he kept with renewed joy the anniversary of his entrance into the cloister. He renewed his profession three times in the course of each day. The cloister was truly the "chosen dwelling of his soul," the house he sincerely loved. Beyond the cloister was the turbulent world, for which he felt an insurmountable disgust. He would fain

---

[48] "Note-book," February 7, 1903.
[49] "Thoughts," CVI, *and many other passages in his notes at this period.*
[50] St. Benedict, Prologue.

never leave his cell, but plunge himself in recollection, so deep a recollection that never again might his thoughts or his heart turn aside from the sole Object of his love."[51]

Whatever might be his other sufferings, Brother Pius never left off any of his mortifications. He courageously wore the hair shirt for whole days together, even during the walks; as far as obedience permitted, he made use of other instruments of penance known to all religious. He kept faithfully to his little acts of piety, such as the recitation of the "Veni Creator" in the morning on coming down to the choir, and in the evenings on going to his cell, the meditation of the reposeful strophes of the "Veni Sancte Spiritus." But all this was done with great liberty of spirit. "Does it not cost you a great deal?" asked a Brother one day, "to be so regular in making the Way of the Cross?" "If it really cost me anything, I should not do it," was the reply. This was saying too much, but we can read between the lines. When grace impels, it imparts a "go" to every action and puts them above the caprices of nature.

Generally speaking, these "practices of devotion" were rare. Brother Pius, as a monk, found in the Divine Office enough and ample wherewith to keep alive his piety and maintain his union with God. The *Opus Dei*, as St. Benedict calls it[52] remained for him the chiefest work. Not only did he give to this, as in duty bound, the first place in all his exercises,[53] but his soul drew more and more abundant supplies of spiritual nourishment from that ever pure and never failing source.

This became easier than ever to him after he was appointed Master of Ceremonies. In the monastery this functionary has daily duties, especially at the Conventual Mass; and on many occasions the Office calls for particular gifts necessary to exercise it well—foresight and

---

[51] *Letter of April* 16, 1904.
[52] *Rule*, ch. XLIII.
[53] "Nihil operi Dei praeponatur." Ibid.

He Studies Theology

decision, tact and self-control. These qualities harmonised with each other in Brother Pius, and for three years he fulfilled his charge, to the satisfaction of all. One thing is worthy of remark which is a subject of admiration, that he joined with recollection a lively attention to his duties; he knew how to give a soul to the ceremonies themselves, as he also knew how to discover the fruitful strength which lies under their symbolism. This charge greatly disposed Brother Pius to receive Holy Orders worthily, as it obliged him to acquire for himself an extended and exact knowledge of the rites of the Church, as well as allowing him to approach nearer to the Altar and to cooperate more actively in the holy actions. Usually, promotion to Holy Orders follows closely after the solemn Profession. Dom Pius, as he must henceforth be called, was successively ordained subdeacon, May 23, 1902, deacon, August 7, 1902, and priest, August 30, 1903.

But it was the atmosphere of mystic suffering in which he lived, that prepared him, far more than even his post of Master of Ceremonies, for receiving the graces of the Priesthood, and these accentuated in his soul the state of abandon and immolation.

The subdiaconate was instrumental in showing to the young levite the grandeur of the holy Mass. We must here quote one of his "Thoughts" which shows us the place which the supreme event of the Death of a God holds in the history of the human race, and especially in the existence of a monk. Before he started for Malines, where he was to receive the first of the Major Orders, Dom Pius made an earnest and ardent prayer to Jesus and His holy Mother.

"Grant that I may never approach the holy Altar without recollecting the sublime character of the Act I am to perform there."[54]

Three months later, Dom Pius was raised to the dignity of the priesthood. With deep but calm delight he pondered over the closer

---

[54] "Note-book," March 22, 1902.

union which the ineffable character would establish between himself and Christ. But none the less did he tremble at uniting himself to the Divine Victim.

Whilst embracing his new ministry with ardour, he "felt deeply the consequence of ordination generously accepted." Thus he writes:[55]

> I am looking forward to an abundant outpouring of the Holy Spirit into my poor soul which I abandon to Him so completely, that this Divine Spirit will do whatever He wills therein. My joy is very great, and yet I must accept this ordination as a painful thing....I feel how entirely we are one with Christ at the moment of fulfilling a priestly function. The priest, as Christ Himself, continues the role of the Immolator and the Victim.
>
> And how terrible that immolation is! Still, it must be accepted without reserve if I am to present myself for imposition of hands. I must be willing to bear whatever suffering love may see fit to lay upon me. Yes! indeed, when the soul enters only a little into this mystery, it cannot but fear. Christ Himself was in agony at the prospect of the Passion.
>
> And again he writes,[56] "when one has taken those first steps into the sanctuary which lead to the holy way of the priesthood, that divine vocation more often opens a view of sufferings to the terror-stricken soul, rather than that of honours. But a fervent soul accepts this dolorous ministry, which makes him feel, beforehand, the sacrifice of the Cross."

The final step now remained, that of the priesthood. We read in the "Thoughts" as follows:[57]

> To become a priest is to be chosen by the Holy Spirit to follow Christ to Gethsemane and to Calvary. The priest who realises

---

[55] "Thoughts," LXXXVI.
[56] "Thoughts," LXXXVI.
[57] "Thoughts," LXXXVI.

the spirit of his state, is a man of sorrows; he carries the burden of souls, that is to say, their griefs, their weaknesses and their sins.

Being abundantly enlightened from heaven, Dom Pius was penetrated with the conviction of the responsibilities belonging to those who share Christ's work of Redemption; and he experienced the truth of the words of St. Gregory of Nazianzen that "no one is ordained priest with a light heart."

"When one walks towards a place so terrible as the Sanctuary, and above all, as the Altar," he said, "one walks resolutely, but counts one's steps."

For the last two years Dom Pius had his eyes fixed on the date of his Ordination which drew near rapidly. At the beginning of the last year of his studies, he confides to his "Note-book," "the real, great, and sole desire of my heart in view of the priesthood, is, that from thenceforward my will may be entirely one with that of God, and utterly transformed by the Holy Spirit."[58]

In the month of April he went into Retreat under the protection of Mary, and writes in the "Note-book" (April 18, 1903).

> On the eve of my ordination, Oh! beloved Lady! draw my mind apart from all earthly preoccupations; hide me in the Presence of God, in order that He may look upon me, and that His divine Look may penetrate the depths of my heart, and pierce it deeply with the wound of love....Thou knowest the fathomless humility required for the priesthood; grant me, from today, to live in a state of recollection and lead me, Thyself, with a Mother's hand.

---

[58] "God's Note-book," October 11, 1902.

Indeed, there was no time to be lost; the divine Master redoubled His action, and hastened His young deacon in purifying himself for the great day; he writes to a companion:

> Our Lord has given me a glimpse of what has to be put to death within my poor soul, and it is not a very cheering sight. And then, if we truly are priests indeed, we must remain immolated during our whole lifetime.[59]

To Dom Pius, annihilation of self and personal sanctity seemed inseparable from the sacerdotal character. To celebrate the holy Mass, to perform the august functions of the priest without first having "crucified himself," would be to claim the honour, whilst refusing the pain, and so to expose himself to the wrath of God. Fortunately, God, Who Himself makes choice of His ministers, is able to confer upon them a perfection proportioned to the dignity of their office.

> In the presence of the supreme Master one can but stand, as a worthless little pitiful creature who has naught else that he should have, but the vehement desire to bend in all things to that Good Master's Will.

Before his ordination Dom Pius took the oath of fidelity to the teaching of the Church in the expressive terms of the profession of Faith of the Council of Trent. After having recapitulated all the treasure of the revealed dogmas, the deacon took his oath, laying his hand on the Gospel.

This Profession of Faith was a great event for Dom Pius, whose experience had already taught him that the soul intent on seeking God alone, finds in the "Credo" an unfailing support.

---

[59] *Letter*, May 12, 1903.

He Studies Theology

Notwithstanding the length of the Symbol of the Council of Trent, he wrote it from end to end with his blood, which he thought unworthy of such an honour. At the foot of the page he added these words:

> Lord, I believe, but help Thou mine unbelief, so that I may hold the mystery of the Faith in a pure heart, and that I may have within me the Mind of Christ Jesus, the One Priest and Victim.

Dom Pius was ordained priest on August 30, 1903, at Maredsous, by Monsignor Heylen, Bishop of Namur, and on the following day said his first Mass, without sensible devotion.

As he had foreseen, the priesthood was to be for him "the power to carry the Cross with the Master," and, some days later, he confides his impression to his "Note-book" (X):

> My Blessed Saviour, since I have been ordained priest, I feel the extreme weakness of my sinful soul much more deeply...it seems to me that Thou wouldst plant and nourish it in the strong soil of suffering. Well,—if it be so—do Thou sustain my weakness.

The studies which follow ordination have for their chief object the preparation for the holy Ministry. Casuistry and moral treatises do not present to the soul the same light and warmth as dogma; but these matters, dry in themselves, are necessary for the healer of souls.

Towards the end of the year Dom Pius went to the Archbishop's residence, for the examination necessary for confessors, and then he returned to Maredsous.

In August, 1904, he wrote to his father:

> I returned from Malines some days ago. The examination seems to have been satisfactory, judging by the powers granted me. The best part is, that for the moment I am at peace with my books, happy to be back in my monastery, and preparing to receive some Obedience. What that may be, I know not yet.

Chapter VI

The Teaching Monk

*They cannot remain insensible to divine charity
whilst I burn to see it grow in their hearts.*
—"Letter," September 5, 1904

The priestly character is an active power which demands to be used; and in this as in all else, Christ has pointed out the way. It is true, that not all who share in His priesthood are called to lay down, like the good shepherd, their life for the sheep; but, at least they ought to be "wearied with labours and pains" in the corner of His vineyard assigned to them by the divine Master, as St. Gregory says in his life of St. Benedict.[60]

It was with just these convictions that Dom Pius returned to his dear Abbey of Maredsous. With eyes fixed on God "as the eyes of a servant on the hand of his master"[61] waiting until the Divine Will should manifest Itself, and ready to accomplish that Will, with consecration both of soul and body, without ever failing. Full well he

---

[60] c. VI.
[61] P. CXXII, v. 2.

knew that he should fulfil his mission imperfectly and be false to the tradition of his Order unless he joined action with contemplation, and made the first subservient to the second. To his prayers he added work: *Ora et labora*. Activity in the monastery is many-sided and of large scope, the Benedictine Rule not limiting in any way the field of labour to those who profess it.[62]

Dom Pius, in the meantime did not look ahead, nor wonder what his mission should be. As a monk, he had given *himself* up once for all, believing that to his Abbot, enlightened by divine grace, and knowing the circumstances and the brethren well, belonged the right of declaring what God expects of His servants, so that He may in all things be glorified.[63] Respecting the destinies of all, it lies with the Abbot to set their feet in the direction peculiar to each one, disposing of all his sons as he sees fit, so as to stir each one's initiative, to develop their talents and encourage their efforts.

This principle, which takes so much account of individual capacity, is at once supple and strong: the character, respected as far as it ought so to be, can expand spontaneously, whilst Obedience remains the spring of its action. It will be seen later, that in Dom Pius, the spirit of initiative and devotion to Obedience harmonised with that love which was the soul of his life. This vital principle gave a consistency to all his activity, marking it with a powerful character of unity.

---

[62] This, it may be well to say as we go on, explains to a great extent, the marvellous spread and fruitfulness of the works undertaken by the Benedictine Order in the course of its fourteen centuries of existence. No difficulties have been able to hinder its activity, and no branch of usefulness has been left uncultivated.

"The historian of the Monastic Order," says Montalembert in his "Monks of the West," vol. VII, p. 113, "may fearlessly challenge his rivals to cite any class of men whatever, which, at any epoch has rendered services to human society and its varied interests that can be compared, in number and in importance, to those which the world owes to monks."

[63] Reg. c. LVI.

The Teaching Monk

In October, 1904, he was named prefect at the College; his talents lay more in the cultivation of souls than in the role of professor. Very soon he acquired a surprising influence over the pupils, and revealed himself as a leader of the young. It is not enough that the prefect should keep strict watch over his flock; he should also be their adviser and as a father to their youth. He should aim at drawing them out of the deplorable moral isolation in which they often live exposed to many bad influences.

Dom Pius understood his charge and entered upon it zealously. With a sure glance he drew up an outline of conduct for himself, which he summed up on his deathbed, two years later, in a letter written at that time.

> In my opinion the programme of a good prefect can be comprised in a few words:
> 1. To be a monk DETACHED FROM EVERYTHING.
> 2. To love the children very much, and quite impartially, and to let them see this.
> 3. To show them very great CONFIDENCE, for they are generally good, but to watch over them *loyally* and *actively*, so as to know as much as possible all that is going on, for childhood is frail and apt to fall.
> 4. Kindly and by degrees to exact *perfect discipline*, which should be observed more by the feeling of duty than by fear of punishment.
>
> In these few lines, which require much explanation, I lay before you my profound convictions, the result of experience. The ideal they trace is one very difficult to attain and I am very far from having realised it myself, but it is the end I aim at as prefect. The influence thus gained over the pupils is a true and healthy influence. I should like to show you the letters the dear children have written to me whom I have had to do with—do not pass on this paper, I beg of you, nor tell others about it; they would think that I "hold forth" well!

The results of Dom Pius' methods and thoughts are shown to us more clearly by his life than by his written words. His leading thought was truly that he must be a "monk detached from all things," and it was thus that he entered upon his duties. Freed from trivial preoccupations, he saw only the eternal side of things, "the general good to be obtained, even at the expense of one's own little self…may that little self disappear and be forgotten in order that good may be done and the glory of God alone increase."[64]

In his devotion to his dear School, Dom Pius now found that "if divine love has its follies, so must also the love of our neighbour." His zeal, nevertheless, was not suffered to lead him to differ from the views of those who directed the common work. Just as the little novice had been docile to the voice of his Father-Master, so was the prefect supple in the hands of the Rector of the College: beyond the authority of this last, Dom Pius never allowed himself to take the initiative. Before all else he sought the *general* good, and to influence the mass of the pupils. Rather than acting on isolated individuals, he preferred to set in motion a current that should be capable of carrying the stagnant elements along with it. In this he succeeded perfectly. With his heart and mind in the upper ether, he knew none the less how to knead the terrestrial dough with his hands! It was all the same to him, when once he saw the means of action, whether it was by the Society of St. Vincent of Paul—or by the various works attached to a Guild,—or by games of cricket and football. He knew how to make use of each and all. Whilst, as to the poor people who dwelt near the Abbey, Dom Pius did not allow his other interests to prevent him from being at the head of charitable movements for them, which he undertook and at his own cost, too.

---

[64] "Note-book," May 25, 1905.

The Teaching Monk

A workman on the railway had his arm frightfully burnt, so that the limb was one running sore. Every day for two months Dom Pius poulticed the wound with tender solicitude until it was completely cured. A witness of this assures us, "a mother could not have treated her own child more lovingly." Another time, it was an unfortunate, homeless family who begged shelter. Dom Pius set to work with the elder boys, spade in hand; they dug the foundations for a humble cottage, a collection was set on foot, and soon the family was installed in a neat abode. Animated by his example, the children learned "to devote themselves to the needy, with impartial minds and unfailing charity." The little circle of boys privileged to be members of the Society of St. Vincent of Paul, was penetrated by the spirit of the Saint's invaluable "Manual," and they thus early understood and enjoyed the happiness of meeting christians "with one heart and one soul." When their studies were ended they might return to Maredsous, and though Dom Pius would no longer be there, they would find their way amongst the cottages they had visited with him, and, carrying some little acceptable present to their old friends, they would repeat, and joyfully hear the oft-repeated and sweet refrain: "Ah! Brother Pius! what a good father he was!"

To these house-to-house visits of charity, other good works were soon added, notably Conferences for men and a savings bank destined for the purchase of houses for the workmen. This last enterprise caused much anxiety to the young monk, who had no experience in money matters…nor in the greed of mortals for coin! Even on his deathbed he wrote innumerable letters to clear up complicated money matters.

At the moment when he was leaving Maredsous, he was on the point of handing over a house to its happy proprietor, and he wrote.

> I beg you, being at hand, to follow up this job—so as to give twenty francs at the end of each month, telling N. that things are

going on quite well, and that, probably, he will have possession of his capital, as well as his last payment of interest, before the month of March. This business has cost me so much trouble and anxiety that I dread to see it go wrong.

The Conferences for men were held every month in one of the halls of the College. Dom Pius, here again was the moving spirit, and took upon himself to conduct the opening meetings. We find one address on Lourdes given by him with lantern views: another on the different parties in Belgian politics—this last was given with the intention of spreading an electoral tract. But as far as possible, the talks were to be given by the pupils. "Our young people must make a start; our work has prospered thus far, and I think it very important that it should be kept going in a lively way, as well by our boys as by the men. I think it will do as much good to the one set as to the other, if it be kept up in a spirit of simplicity and mutual charity."

Dom Pius it was, too, who realised the idea which had been suggested by the "Messagère de St. Benoît," of founding a "Farm-chapel" in the Congo. His schemes for various collections, including stamps, old metals, silvered papers and other wastes is still in practice. This enterprise was the specialty of the youngest pupils who were very zealous in gathering together such trifling odds and ends.

Convinced that, among children as well as among their elders, nothing is really likely to succeed well without a spirit of joy and cheerfulness of heart which drives away the blues; the prefect applied himself to "maintaining good humour" among his little company. Being himself a good player at athletic games, he organised a team for football, arranged for tennis and other sports. All these were formed as *Clubs*, or special associations, each having its own rules and cashbook. "This," he writes, "is, in my opinion the best way of organising these games; the personal initiative of the boys finds scope there.

The Teaching Monk

They are the first to demand order in their respective Clubs, and are proud of them: they play with the greatest spirit."

Nor did Dom Pius' activity end there. He liked good organisation, which helps to keep up order and regularity. If he saw any part of the work defective, his ingenious and practical mind soon found a way to improve it. He set up a motor which worked several engines, thus economising personal labour. The department for dispensing medicines being insufficient, he arranged with the dispenser for its improvement. Thus more and more he spread that "good spirit" which makes a college to be like a united family—pure, industrious, loving, and full of piety.

Mutual confidence reigned alike between the Master and the children: this was a matter of tradition, but with Dom Pius it became *filial* confidence. At their own suggestion the pupils promised him never to break a rule, and they kept their word. Such a proof of good will and energy delighted the young prefect, who profited by the occasion to say a word of good advice. For, as he well knew that much can be done by a general movement, so he knew, too, how to influence the individual at the proper moment. To this delicate work he brought the wisdom and experience of riper years. Nothing seemed to him more beautiful than a young pure soul under the action of grace. Thus he writes to one of his brethren.

> I understand so well what you say about souls! How lovely it is to follow their growth, to fight together with them—sometimes against them! To teach them divine love and hatred of self! does it not surprise you to find how light and yet how sure a touch is required in the hand that has to cultivate souls? It needs a rare gift of devotion to adapt oneself to all requirements and await the hour of grace—to know the right moment to cut short when necessary; to feel when to sympathise and when to rejoice with the soul. For my own part, I grieve that I can so seldom touch the

children's souls in an intelligent manner! They ought to possess greater self-knowledge—but how few there are in the world who do really know themselves!

Dom Pius scarcely dares to say it—yet it is really his thought—that, in dealing with young people one must try to fill the place that the mother naturally holds in her family. Without the sweet influence of maternal affection, the child loses the delicacy of feeling, which is seldom now to be met with; he becomes rough and intractable. The best part of his soul shrivels, dries up, and even, alas! grows corrupt. Now, Dom Pius writes in his "Note-book":

> My heart is full of tenderness for my dear children: I give them my whole self. But I feel that a prefect, however affectionately devoted he may be, has always a certain stiffness, a something official in his look, which is enough to hold back the full, spontaneous confidences which would otherwise gush out, giving the superior a chance of much power for good.[65]

Again, we read in a letter to a friend,

> the best weapon for the fight—a weapon that is always strong and ever sure of victory—is an unbounded love of God and of His holy Will. My own conviction is, that I only do good to any of the children entrusted to me, in the degree of my love for them.

After this, do we need to ask what it was that Dom Pius sought to instil into the children? He tells us, himself, saying that what he wishes, is "to teach them to love, for he who knows how to love, can do great things." Now, these *great things* consist above all, in performing well the duties of each one's state in life.

---

[65] "Note-book," May 23, 1906.

The Teaching Monk

We read in the journal of one of the little college boys: "the sense of duty is what makes a man. I want to become a great saint by doing my duty."

Generally, in giving advice, Dom Pius limited himself with a few words to the point. Once, when a soul came to him in great discouragement he only said: "True strength can be found nowhere but in Jesus Christ; go and communicate often."

A soft character got a bit of advice exactly suited. "You should mortify yourself. Mortification confirms the love of God and establishes the absolute kingdom of the will in us."—To another he said, "the Food of our souls is Holy Communion. Let us receive It in order to love much, and let us love without reserve so that we may receive It worthily."

Sometimes he spoke at greater length. Once he said:

> "The divine Gardener cares for these little flowers with excessive love…let us always bask under the action of this divine Sun of Charity: I mean to say, let us always act through love—and then all we do will be like sweet incense mounting up to heaven. This is quite easy when done with a good grace, and is always very pleasing to our dear Lord, and full of consolation for ourselves. Let us give our hearts to this dear good Master; our whole hearts and all our affections; this is a work of great profit; for love finds in it immense strength, without losing any of its power and tenderness towards those who surround us," then he added, "if you take in these little things, and practice them well, you will soon find that you are running by the simple way of love as if in play along the path of true holiness, and drawing very near to God."

And now pray, what is becoming of the hidden life of the young prefect,—that life that formerly absorbed him—now that he spends himself from morning till night among his noisy boys?

Certainly, it was none the less intense now. If he had lost his intimacy with God, Dom Pius would have thought himself a monk no longer. Even at this time, exteriorly so full of duties, the "seeking after God," which is characteristic of the monk,[66] remained the leading note of all his life's harmony. His constant care was to prevent himself from being carried away by his work, for Dom Pius knew well that work, although essential in the life of a monk, must be subordinate to contemplation. Obedience is his starting point, but his food for the way is prayer. He writes:

> I have been asking myself whether I ought not to put narrower limits to my activity? what soul that truly seeks God, does not have painful doubts on this point, sometimes?

Convinced, as he was, of the fruitlessness of all purely human effort, and persuaded that union with God is the condition for efficacious ministry, he aspires to that enviable state wherein God attracts the activity of our nature to Himself, in order to leave us no power but that of acting in concert with Him.

> "So many people," he writes to a friend, "rush about and make a great noise uselessly, because they work without God, or against Him. On the other hand, how beautiful and consoling it is to consider the influence, deep though hidden, of the man who acts as a true Christian, that is, under the power of grace. When a soul unites itself to its God in prayer, it ends by being 'clothed upon' with the very Power of God."

All the leisure time at his own disposal, Dom Pius consecrated to contemplative prayer. A witness of his actions tells us: "every evening, between 5 and 6 o'clock, I found the Father in prayer in the College

---

[66] Holy Rule, *Prologue*, and ch. LVIII.

Chapel. His appearance was more than reverent, it was angelic. I do not know how he could pray there like that!"

Nor was it less impressive to see him at the Altar: The Brothers who served his Mass have never lost the remembrance. The Holy Sacrifice was his very life.

> "How many times," he wrote, "when I went up to the Altar heavy hearted—feeble in soul and weary in body—have I not come down consoled and strengthened!"

The mysteries of the Liturgical year always furnished the best food for his religious soul, and in his letters to friends, we find allusions to all the Festivals, from Christmas to All Saints. On these occasions he liked to be in touch with those specially united to him by the bonds of affection and prayer.

From the prefects' desk he writes to one of his friends, at the beginning of Advent (December 3, 1905).

> I have just finished saying Vespers of the 1st Sunday in Advent, and closed the Breviary. The admirable Liturgy for this season is too rich in graces for me to resist wishing that you yourself may fathom the Divine wealth contained therein. When I am very penetrated by deep impressions, I always wish to tell you about them. Now, I must say, that nothing appeals to me more than the Advent Offices, and (I tell you this quite simply and in all sincerity,) I believe it is because of my great yearning after union with Him Who Alone can fill the emptiness of our poor hearts. The prayers of the Church during Advent are all so many longing sighs and cries of hope! They respond so well to the cravings of the soul! How happy we are to be able to join our feeble voices to those powerful invocations!

Still, Dom Pius was willing to grant that he was not always "in the right key to chime in with the ceremonies of the Church. For *that*, one needs to be very recollected; and often one has not the strength needed to rise to the level of the true life of the soul."

Formerly, when free from all cares, he found a peaceful and unfathomable joy in spending a whole feast day in the Offices and chants of the Liturgy: but now, he could but seldom find freedom from his duties so as to think of nothing but God. He writes to a companion:

> During this Christmas night, I was obliged to leave the Office, to wake the little boys: at the Communion (which occupied the Bishop half an hour to distribute), I found time to make my prayer: and this was almost the only interval of leisure during the whole day that was given me to recollect myself in God! Do not think, though, that this saddened me. My soul is *very happy*, because there is always, in the depths, a sincere longing for God. I know it is He Who feeds it there and will realise my desires some day, if, by His Grace, I remain faithful to Him.

Dom Pius' private journal had to be suspended during the whole of the two busy years he spent at the College. From September 24, 1904, to May 26, 1906, "God's Note-book" is blank—and in the "Aspirations and Thoughts" we find little more than one page, entitled "The Beloved Land." This he composed on returning from a visit to his childhood's friend, which seemed to be specially arranged by Providence! When sending this MS, to his friend, he added a note which we copy, because it applies to everything written by Dom Pius.

> I have tried, as it were to photograph and develop certain impressions that sank very deep into my soul. I find this very difficult, as the things I want to reproduce are spiritual and delicate…words rather betray my meaning…read these notes over musingly, letting your soul rest on them, as mine did when I wrote them.

The Teaching Monk

However, we knew enough of what was passing in his soul; first, there is a letter to his mother, dated June 22, 1906, four days before the fatal attack.

> When one is trying to lead an active life whose centre and springs are in the inmost depths of the soul, ah! *then*, how often things look different! In the same soul there is so much that varies, even in tending towards what is good, that we never seem to find ourselves twice in the same dispositions. And yet, this simple and consistent movement towards God, as it takes possession of the soul more and more, drives out the multiplicity of other feelings; it gathers up the whole life, and reduces it to its simplest expression. In this admirable simplicity it is, indeed, that we find that unvarying, lasting happiness which, ancient as it may be, still constantly reveals itself to us under new aspects.
>
> These thoughts are sinking into me, and there it is that I find the explanation of my happiness and the impossibility of expressing it in words—one word would be enough—you understand it well, this word—this longing that God puts within the heart and on the lips!

But what an astonishing contrast! almost at the same time that he wrote this letter, Dom Pius had jotted down in "God's Note-book" (May 22, 1906).

> I am working hard, perhaps more than I can do, normally. I am told that I am doing good, and I hear this from several quarters. Nevertheless, this appreciation does not affect my soul. Thou, Thyself, oh! my God, never failest to make me feel how utterly worthless is all I do, and how unpardonable is the negligence with which even that little is done! Thou showest me this so strongly, that, for the moment it brings tears to my eyes. I feel myself terribly cast down and crushed before God! I believe,—I *feel* that God is preparing for me something yet more annihilating—and this, not only within my own conscience, but in the sight of men. As it seems to me, this blow will be terrible!

At this time—which was actually the moment, (little as could be foreseen) that was to be the end of his active career—Dom Pius seems to have been divided by two strong emotions—the one joyful—the other laden with suffering. In a letter to a friend he explains this phenomenon in words that scarcely veil the fact that he wrote of his own state; as follows:

> The life of a christian is always made up of a double element. The first is an unfathomable depth of happiness, an unalterable peace, constant joy and exquisite tranquillity. In the inward part of the soul, God dwells and spreads abroad a heavenly atmosphere wherein all solid virtues grow and increase. The other element is suffering, the most precious treasure that can be! which harmonises in a mysterious way with the element of happiness, of which it is the condition. For my own part, nothing comes up to my happiness; but I should think it ephemeral and unreal if I did not feel that in some way it *depends upon trials*: contradictions; failure; weariness; uncertainty—the indifference of others to whom we have been devoted…no other thought lies so deeply, so intensely in my heart as that of suffering.

Dom Pius' external appearance itself betrayed this double state of his soul. Although he was but twenty-six, these last years had aged him remarkably. His mother, coming to see him, was struck at once by this change: she no longer found the youthfulness and freshness she had always seen in her son; but in his face and eyes she could read heavenly things and she admired the beauty that can never fade away.

At this period Dom Pius wrote to one of the monks who had been professed with him, and who now, through illness was away from his monastery. As in this letter he cast a retrospective glance over the seven years of his religious life, we quote it here:

The Teaching Monk

The Feast of our holy Father St. Benedict, my dear Father Barnabas,[67] reminds me of our own Profession seven years ago. All the details live in my memory and came back freshly today, when Father Abbot received the vows of two young monks. If my effusions are not too much for you—I will confide in you that I was particularly struck by the words in the Ceremonial...*et non confundas me ab expectatione mea.*[68]

When once our life has been really given to God, is it possible to spend seven years in monastic life without suffering? I don't believe it is possible...and you can endorse my opinion with unquestionable authority. Ah! well—notwithstanding—my whole soul protests that God has not disappointed my expectations, but, on the contrary, He has surpassed my hope! Yes—there are dark hours—toilsome days—but these are the very food of joy, How good God is! and how well He must love us really, to give us something to suffer!

Having escaped the deceptions of life, Dom Pius will neither have to know the bitterness of death.

---

[67] Dom Barnabas Comblin, who died at Maredsous. September 4, 1908.
[68] These words are sung by the Novice after having read the form of his Vows, and are part of the Ceremony of the Monastic Profession according to the Rule of St. Benedict, ch. LIII. They are, as it were, by contrast, the pendant to those other words which immediately precede "Receive me, oh! Lord, according to Thy Word."—"*Suscipe me Domine secundum eloquium Tuum et vivam.*"

Chapter VII

The 'Final Grace'

*When will that happiest of days come,
when charity shall have confirmed
our souls in God? I would not wish to
put it off to the distant future.*

—"Letter," September 24, 1901

There is one page in Dom Pius' "Note-book," on which he has written down the memorable dates of his life or perhaps, it would be better to say, the long list of divine favours of which he was the happy object. Here it is:

Great Graces Received

Baptism	April 21, 1880
First Confession	***
Confirmation	March 17, 1889
First Communion	March 23, 1890
Entrance into Religion	December 8, 1897
Noviciate	March 18, 1808
Simple Profession	March 21, 1899

Minor Orders. Low Sunday	April 9, 1899
Theological studies at Louvain	October 1900
Solemn Consecration to the Divine Word	March 25, 1901
Union of my heart with that of Mary	June 23, 1901
Solemn Profession	March 21, 1902
Sub-diaconate	May 23, 1902
Diaconate in Octave of the Assumption	1902
Priest's Orders. Feast of the Angel Guardians	August 30, 1903
Prefect at the college	October 1904
Hœmorrhage	June 27, 1906

We have already passed these "Great Graces" in the review, with the exception of the last, which began on the evening of June 27. Dom Pius had been superintending the boys who were going to bed and had himself retired to his cubicle at the end of the dormitory; when, on bending down, he was seized with a violent attack of blood-spitting. On the morrow he writes of this event in "God's Note-Book."

June 28, 1906

Last evening I spit blood for the first time. It was a bad attack and I felt very done up, and doubtful whether I should survive. But this morning I am rather better and, thank God, was able to say Mass easily. I hoped to have got over my troubles after a good day's rest, but it is not so at all. Indeed, I feel myself, that I need some rest. This is given me, and, to make it as complete as possible, I am kept in the Abbey Infirmary. When I entered the Infirmary, I felt something of that *chill* sensation which is inspired by all those matter of fact arrangements made for the sick when death is drawing near. But the profound peace and calm which reigns around me allow my mind to dwell naturally on Thee, my God. I am quite happy and the only thing I dread is that I may not be able to say Mass. If, however, I should be forbidden to do so, I will submit from the bottom of my heart; as I wish to do, in everything else that may be prescribed. I rest so completely in Thy Hands that I do not wish even to think about what may be done for me, nor of what may happen.

May my love for Thee, oh! Best-beloved, weak as it is, make all things work together for my good—that is to say, for Thy Glory in me.

That Mass of June 28 was to be his last: and the deprivation of the holy Sacrifice marks the first stage of that complete work of spoliation which death was to complete.

Weeks passed…months passed…the Feast of the Assumption of his Lady, of All Saints, of the following Christmas—and still Dom Pius' great hope was vain. On two occasions he was on the point of going up to the Altar—everything was ready overnight for the Celebration on the following day, and each time a fresh attack nailed the invalid to his bed. "It is God Himself," said he, "Who *suspends* His unworthy servant."[69]

On July 3, Dom Pius was taken to his parental home, as it was hoped that in his native air, his cure might be effected sooner so that he could resume his post at the College in the following October. It was a sad departure. His pupils lined the passage near to the playground, to wish him "come back soon" but he could only reply by tears.

The journey did not cause any return of the illness, but, once at his home, Dom Pius felt he was an exile from his dear monastery and confided these burning and melancholy lines to a scrap of paper:

---

[69] Alluding to the ecclesiastical term "suspension" against an unworthy priest, which "suspends" him from saying Mass.

> As the rivers flow to the sea—as the flower lifts its head to the sun—as the timid fawn seeks the deepest solitudes—so does my soul ever tend, rushing to Thee, oh! my Lord! For it is Thou only Who canst satisfy my soul with Thy splendour, it is in Thee alone that it can plunge—losing itself in the divine solitudes which Thy Presence creates in it: "Ecce elongavi fugiens et mansi in solitudine."

After grave consultation, the doctors gave it as their opinion, that pulmonary congestion of a serious nature was present, and ordered the patient to be kept in a recumbent position. So he remained in bed—and for long months! Here, however, Dom Pius passed his time with a regularity that was truly monastic, arranging his various occupations of reading, letter-writing and meals, as nearly as possible in accordance with the hours kept in the Abbey; and he made all converge towards the hours for the divine Office, from which he would retrench nothing. He considered that, as a monk, his dearest treasure lay there, and he wished to lose no part of it.

Of course, these could not be the "good, well-filled days" of the past; but for an invalid his occupations were amply enough. Someone having found them over-much, reproached Dom Pius with not taking care of himself as he should do: his answer was straightforward.

> You think I am doing too much, and ought not to say my Hours. The only rule possible for me now, is scrupulous obedience to the doctor's orders. I submit to him every item of my work—I tell him and show him all I read: he allows me in so much (childish activity) as helps me to Sleep at night, and have some appetite for food.

Faithful to the principle that had guided his whole life, the monk applied himself to being *a good invalid*; therein lay the duty of his state of life, the Obedience he owed to the formal intention of his superior. Besides this, he promised and practiced exact obedience to the medical man and to the nursing Sister. Sometimes he could not keep his food down; but a word was enough to make him take it, though the necessary result followed. He never showed any preference for one thing before another, and the Sister had to give him an express order before he would pronounce any opinion.

Thinking to please Dom Pius, some light literature had been given him, but he would have none of it and asked that his dear theological treatises might be brought, the same he had studied at Louvain with so much profit. He seemed, on the Sill of Eternity to enjoy, even more than before, these mysterious dogmas, the glorious realities of which he would so soon contemplate, face to face! He read Holy Scripture assiduously, as well as the best spiritual writers—St. Augustine, St. Jerome, St. Gertrude and St. Mechtilde for whom he had a great devotion, as well as for St. Theresa and St. Francis de Sales, who succeeded each other at his bedside.

Often, in the course of his reading, he might be seen absorbed in prayer, with joined hands, motionless, his face illumined with celestial Serenity. The two Sisters who nursed Dom Pius, both declared they had never seen anyone pray like he did, and they were much edified by being with him.

A part of each day was devoted to manual labour, and, looking about to find some little restful occupation of the kind, the former Director of the Conferences of St. Vincent bethought himself of making woollen comforters for his poor people, pleasing himself with picturing their joy at receiving such gifts. The Sister, also, imitating the good example of her patient, began to make garments for those in need, and as they worked, they chatted a bit. Dom Pius, surrounded by his relations, gave free course to his cheerful temper.

His priestly soul, ever eager to speak of God, found the best way to exercise his zeal now lay in his correspondance, and he wrote several letters each day: sometimes to his religious brethren, or his poor people, his pupils, or his personal friends. The extent of his influence on others can be seen by his letters.

Here, for instance, he writes to an invalid whom he was in the habit of visiting, and consoles him in, and for God.

> It is indeed true, my dear A., that I feel the most lively interest in you and in your family. Very often my thoughts fly to you, and I suffer more from the enforced absence from my dear poor people than I do from the illness itself. I heard of the sad accidents that have befallen you—and how this grieved me! Indeed—as you say—you did not need further trials. But, at least, what do we know? One thing is certain, in any case God loves us, and all that He does in our regard is done from love. You are quite right to add "May His holy Will be done," and I am greatly comforted that you say this, in the midst of all your sufferings.
>
> We are both suffering, my dear A., let us draw a lesson from it and make the resolution together to serve God all the better.
>
> It seems to me, that both you and I have a grace to thank God for: on my part, that I have been able to go to you, to make your acquaintance and to love you—and on your's—that you know where to find a really true friend, less able to help your material needs than he could wish, but giving to you and yours the consolation and strength of an affection that is deep and devoted in Our Lord.

Dom Pius kept up constant correspondance with the pupils at the College. Their letters are "a delightful recreation" for him: and, if he could not reply to them at the length he would have wished, at least he never failed to send them a few words at once affectionate and helpful. On being told that one of the children recited a

The Final Grace

decade of the Rosary every evening for his intention with his arms stretched in the form of the Cross, Dom Pius at once took up his pen and wrote:

> Do I dare to tell you, my dear child, that I hear you recite *Aves* for me every evening? Before 'my little finger' let us into the secret I could have guessed it—and indeed expected it from *you*! Many thanks! Grateful thanks! I often think of you. You will have gone back into your rather dreamy life—that is all right, but take care that your dreams draw you nearer to God and strengthen you to fulfil all your duties lovingly. It is on that ground that all souls meet who are truly seeking God, and can we not, you and I, reckon ourselves among these?

Another of the pupils had Masses said for the invalid, who writes in return.

> Just a tiny word. *Thank you!* You know what for—our good God told me. I can no longer say holy Mass and this is a great privation. On my part, I pray for you and ask the Divine Master to make your heart like a little bird free as air, and gay as springtime—having no voice except to sing to His glory, what is good and what is pure, isn't that right?—I would not put off telling you this, my dear child, to show you that I am always.
> Yours devotedly.

More than three months passed thus. By degrees the invalid seemed to improve, and there was hope of convalescence, when, quite suddenly, an alarming crisis occurred, more than twelve attacks of hæmorrhage following eachother rapidly on September 17th and 24th: All hope of returning to Maredsous for the opening of the term had to be given up. Here was another rending of the dear ties—a new sacrifice. From that time, Dom Pius felt that among his own pupils he should be but a memory…if they wrote to him, he would joyfully reply, but he could no more take the lead with them for fear of exercising an influence which was no longer his by right. He would not do the least thing towards seeming to keep an office which Providence had taken from him so suddenly. And thus he wrote:

> From the day when God no longer chooses to make use of our weakness, further activity is worse than useless. It is necessary to be fully convinced of this, if we would live with hearts detached, joyful and at peace.

Still, once more the attacks quieted down and Dom Pius was able to take up his little occupations. On November 11, as the doctors wished him to try a change of air, he was moved without danger to his maternal grandfather's house, in the province of Limbourg. Soon afterwards, a third and more terrible attack came on, worse, than any of the former. Two penciled notes, written by the invalid himself with regard to his health, tell us sufficiently how severe the attack had been.

> November 23, 1906
>
> I scribble a few words—flat in my bed. This last week has been no better than the one in September from the 17th to the 24th. I spit blood almost every day, and the fever never leaves me. It is difficult to appear cheerful—as I am not allowed to speak, and am very exhausted bodily. But I am quite happy in myself and our Good God is only too kind to me! The crisis will pass off.

And again, a few days later.

> December 4, 1906
>
> After a fortnight of it, the temperature is going down. The fever ran high—over 40°—but for the moment I am normal, and

the bleeding has ceased. But how many things have been done to produce this effect! Injections and engotine, sinaplasms, hot bottles to my feet and bandages on arms and legs! I have greatly suffered, but it is all a loving gift from God. I wish you and very Rev. Father Prior a holy Advent. The lovely chants of the season sound in my ears, and it would be *paradise* if I could assist at some of the Offices! But the trial is not over yet, and when I think of all the wounds of my poor soul that need cleansing, it seems to me, much more suffering will be necessary. It is true, we have the sufferings of Christ to encourage us—to which it suffices to unite our little ones.

Dom Pius' strong physical nature seemed to assert itself again—but, this time, he was doubtful of himself.

"When shall I have finished with these many attacks?" he writes: "the doctors give *doubtful* hopes, and I have no hope, except that God orders all wisely and that we do not know what His adorable designs may be. Shall I tell you my own opinion?—it is, that all this trial is so completely the work of God, and I find myself so entirely in His divine Hands, that no one can possibly tell whether I am near the end yet, of my 'Day of the Cross.' May God be blessed for leading me to it."

Three weeks went by before the illness made its final assault, and the moral results of six long months of suffering are made known to us by memories of some quiet conversations, and a few letters during these last days. More than ever, Dom Pius felt that:

> there is nothing—neither place, nor work, nor any other thing that can fill and satisfy the heart, except the love of God and of our neighbour.

Through the windows of his sickroom he could see the sun, the rain and snow-storms succeeding each other, but without in any way affecting him. And the thought occurred to him that it is thus with a soul stedfast in the peace and love of God, in regard to the passing things of the world. Earth withdraws—not only with its vanities and attractions, but even with its holiest compensations—the holy Sacrifice of the Mass—the Monastery—the works of obedience and the joys of sacrifice. To the monk, two things only remain; "a consuming need of possessing God, and the consciousness of his own nothingness in the sight of the Divine Majesty."

During several years this twofold ideal had been ever on the increase; the last trial would intensify it yet more.

If we are to believe the last entries in "God's Note-book," Dom Pius was assailed on his deathbed by temptations far more painful to him than physical sufferings.

It is true that he never committed a great sin in his life, but he did not need so much as that to alarm him. At the thought that he might, perhaps, have offended God, grief took possession of his heart and filled his eyes with tears.

> "Believe me," he said to one of his brethren, "I am not speaking exaggeratingly when I say that my heart is heavy when I realise the true state of my soul. The facts oblige me to this humility: so many miseries would make me unbearable to anyone who could see them."[70]

He was not surprised that God saw fit to leave him in a state of aridity. On December 5 he wrote a long letter in pencil to Dom Marmion, of which the following is the principal passage:

> I am not in the least surprised that the divine Master does not yet open His Heart to me: I do feel, in all sincerity, utterly

---

[70] NOTE-BOOK, July 15, 1906.

unworthy of it, and this conviction keeps me in great peace. I have no consolation in my soul; my faults are ever before my eyes, and yet I have no other desire than Christ. I will suffer, if God so wills, all my life long. But when will He come for whom we so long and suffer after—and sigh for Him all our life long? God gives me courage, peace and contrition: when will He give me Jesus?

I confide to you all these thoughts, that weigh upon and pursue me always—the only resource I find is in complete abandonment.

At length (January 1, 1907) Dom Pius opened his manuscript-book of "Thoughts and Aspirations."

It was for the last time, and the words he wrote were these: "Here below, the great mysteries of love are deep abysses of suffering. In the soul, love does not become truly a mystery until the day when it touches the innermost windings and folds; and, without inflicting very painful burns, the sacred fire never touches these depths."

When he wrote these last lines, the invalid was already in the grasp of death: general discomfort oppressed him, appetite failed and sleep had taken flight. The fever continued to increase, and frequent shivering fits accompanied the rise of temperature, together with stiffness and violent pains in the legs. There was evidently a serious complication. His chief doctor now whispered the word "meningitis"—and following events confirmed his opinion.

On January 12 Dom Pius became prostrated and stupified—violent pains in his head, frequent sickness and other symptoms gave rise to fears that before long, unconsciousness would set in. That same evening, his brother administered the Last Sacraments to Dom Pius, who received them with great piety. Holding the Crucifix, he kissed the Wounds of our Saviour, and drew from them that sacred Wine, from which he had been weaned so long, saying, "It is like...when I drank the Chalice of the Precious Blood."

Dom Marmion, watching by the bedside of Dom Pius, wrote to one of his relations on January 16.

> To tell you quite openly what I think of our dear Dom Pius, I believe there is no hope. Unless our Lord does not work a miracle, I think that his illness will have the upper hand. However, *nondum statim finis!* Yesterday I gave him the Blessing of St. Maurus—it was that Saint's Feast—and this morning I gave him Holy Communion. Dom Pius suffers much in his whole body, but most of all in his head: Meningitis is feared. He was so delighted to see me. His patience and resignation are admirable, but he is without a ray of consolation, or the least sensible devotion in God! His is a holy soul.
>
> I am very glad to be here with Dom Jean. The Cross is the root of all fecundity. We have the Cross indeed. *Deo gratias!*

Six days passed thus. Dom Pius, remaining in the same state, his head covered with bags of ice, seemed as if crushed.

On January 19, he recovered from the stupor, and, being slightly delirious, began to talk. There were times when he knew he was not quite himself. "I have read," he said, "in one of Louis Veuillot's works, that illness only really affects a man in so far as the mind is attacked. God permits it to touch my mind, and I feel reduced to nothing."

But the delirium was slight and intermittent, so that Dom Pius spoke spontaneously and reasonably of what was in his heart. He spoke much, and what he said displayed the beauty of his soul, to the great edification of all around him. One day, for instance, someone mentioned that it was Feast of the Holy Name of Jesus, and he said: "All that is necessary for us, is to live in intimacy with Jesus. We ought to live always with Our Lord.—Too often this intimacy is spoken and

The Final Grace

thought of as mawkish, insipid: our devotion ought to be sincere, we must unite ourselves to Christ by a strong, spiritual *Faith*." Then, after a short silence, he went on. "When a soul is united to our Lord, He pursues it; so that He may possess it wholly, He *persecutes* it! How much I have felt this!..."

His speech was affected by the malady, and he spoke hesitatingly—but none the less did he speak of the things of God: even in delirium it was the overflow of his soul that fell from his lips; and he said: "Our devotion ought to be Evangelical—in the spirit of the Church. What immense force there is in St. John's Gospel! That Apostle has, indeed, entered into the secrets of theology. And the Epistles to the Romans and Corinthians are also extraordinarily powerful. But my favourite of all is the Epistle to the Ephesians... the Fathers, too, have the strength of the Gospels....St. Gregory the Great was a pure and simple soul! He understood the *Touch of God*—mysticism. So few people rightly value mysticism, and yet it is *there* that happiness is found...infinite happiness—the contemplation of God."

Whilst Dom Pius spoke thus, several things could be noted down; the close union which ought to reign between souls; the energy which should be brought to the warfare; the purity and joy with which the priest should go up to the Altar—these by turns, were the object of his unconscious preaching.

Nourished as he had been on the beautiful prayers of the Liturgy, he now often used them and loved particularly Solomon's prayer at the Dedication of the Temple. "*Domine Deus, in simplicitate cordis mei laetus obtuli universo....Deus Israel, custodi hanc voluntatem.*"[71]

---

[71] I Paralip., XXIX.

Three days only before his death, he recited the Office of Compline entirely, pausing long on certain words which he repeated with relish: particularly the capitulum *"Tu autem in nobis es Domine…ne derelinquas nos, Domine Deus noster."* (Thou are with us, oh! Lord—do not leave us, Oh! Lord our God) and how impressive on his dying lips were the words of the hymn for that Hour *"Te lucis ante terminum."* (Before the ending of the day, etc.)

That evening he ended his celebration of the Divine Office.

On January 24, after the doctor's visit he became very restless, and told himself the end was near. "I see so clearly," he said, "that I am losing hold of things. The moment is coming when"—and he made a gesture with both hands, signifying the closing of a tomb. Then, drawing himself straighter, he repeated the words, "The things that please Thee, I will do."

At the time, no one understood the great importance Dom Pius attached to these words; and it was only afterwards that the *Act* was found which explained it. That short formula was a renovation of the offering he had made of himself at his solemn Profession.

The great sufferings he was enduring, did not in any way change his good temper, and, near as he was to death, he lost none of his usual calm cheerfulness. His little jokes made those around him smile, but the end was too near at hand to permit this enjoyment.

Paralysis was now creeping gradually, and showed that life could not last long. The invalid's sight was growing dim. When he was asked whether he recognised someone who was near his bed, he answered, with a smile: "Why, yes, it is dear papa! His presence is like the sunshine to me; it does me good and cheers me up."

His family being on their knees beside his bed, Dom Pius, raising his hands, blessed his dear ones with evident joy.

The Final Grace

One of his brothers, asking him: "are you quite at peace?" he answered directly: "Oh! yes, why not?"

During the whole of Saturday January 26, he never ceased saying "Hail Maries," notwithstanding his state of high temperature. A few drops of Lourdes water being given him, as he drank them he said, spontaneously, "Our Lady! I trust in Thee."

On the following day, Septuagesima Sunday, three attacks of inflammation of the brain, complicated by internal hemorrhage came on, following each other at short intervals. About 10 a.m., after the prayers for the dying had been said, Dom Pius lifted up his head twice, and calmly expired.

At that moment his father began a hymn of Thanksgiving, as he had done at Yvan's birth—and—notwithstanding the tears which ran down his cheeks, he said: "Let us all unite in a TE DEUM, which he is singing now in Heaven for the first time."

On that same day Dom Marmion wrote to one of Dom Pius' family: "*Justus germinabit Sicut lilium, et florebit in aeternum ante Dominum.* The divine Bridegroom 'who feeds among the lilies,' has taken our dear Dom Pius, a very beautiful soul, pure and loving, still more purified by long and cruel sufferings, and these without any consolation in the sensible Presence of God. I am sure he will be very powerful in heaven! It is a terrible blow to us all. These trials detach us from earth, and fix our hearts *ubi vera sunt gaudia.*"[72]

---

[72] (From the Prayer for the IV Sunday after Easter).

When the first edition of the Life of Dom Pius appeared, Dom Marmion wrote to Dom Hildebrand de Hemptinne, uncle to Dom Pius and Primate of the Order of St. Benedict: "The *Life* has done me great good: it is so well written, and recalls to my sight a soul that I always loved much in Jesus-Christ." —(*Letter of January* 29, 1919).

The mortal remains of Dom Pius were taken to Maredsous, and, four days later were placed in the apse of the Abbey Church.

May his most pure soul rest in the infinite peace of divine love![73]

---

[73] It has already pleased God to reward the confidence and grant the prayers of several souls who have had recourse to Him through the intercession of Dom Pius (see Appendix III). We beg those who owe any grace to that intervention to make it known to the very *Rev. Father Prior of the Abbey of Maredsous.*

Resting place of Dom Pius de Hemptinne, Cemetery, Maredsous

Abbey of Maredsous

II

Aspirations and Thoughts

An interior soul is a world of holy thoughts and burning aspirations. And all these are known to Thee alone, oh! my God.

Aspirations and Thoughts

1901

I

Why does a pure soul withdraw into solitude? Why should that soul, full of tenderness and affection, so well suited to enjoy the wonders of nature, the works of God's love—why should it bury itself in an austere cloister? By doing so, will it not extinguish the bright and growing flame that was destined to mount up to heaven from the midst of God's beautiful creation? Why should such a one be clothed in a black habit, which, as it is suited to the thought of death, must fill the soul with gloomy feelings, and transform a bright and charming youth into an old age that already verges upon the grave? Why should not the young plant be allowed to grow and bloom there, where it came into being?— there, developing under the dews sent by God, cherished by the warmth of His sunshine, it shot up, and brought forth its first little leaves; why, then, prevent it from expanding? Why dry it, to keep it more securely?...for, after all, is not this what becomes of the most beautiful souls in the cloister?

Indeed! No! That is not what becomes of those privileged souls whom the thoughtless world pities. The pure soul is a fragile plant, so delicate and so tender that Providence cares for it in a very special way—and so, Providence transplants it into a soil where no one can see it any more: Providence waters it with heavenly dew, and warms it with the rays of divine Love. Far from being dried, the buds develop into lovely flower of celestial fragrance which they breathe forth to the heavenly gardener in gratitude for His cares; in its season fruit appears and ripens—the fruit of Life—and the plant continues to blossom and bear fruit during all Eternity. "*They shall flourish like lilies before the Lord forever.*"

It is true, it seems to many people that this beautiful soul has died; they think that, once in a dull cloister she must soon fade and wither.

Can we speak of such mysteries to those who will not understand them? does the flesh ever understand the things of the spirit? They think of the cloistered life of the body—but it is the soul that lives in the monastery! The body may reside there, but it is the soul that lives! The body may even protest; but the soul stays safely in a place so admirably suited for love.

April 1901

II

The most pressing need of a loving soul is to be able to express its love. If it is not understood, it suffers; but the keenest of all pain is when love meets with irony or derision.

April 1901

III

Confidence in some special person may be difficult. But, how can a soul that aims at being all for God, and thinks she is giving Him her heart quite unreservedly, yet refuse to confide in any special person? The reason is, because the soul has not really understood what is included in the act of giving itself to God.

Aspirations and Thoughts

Really, to consecrate one's heart and all one's being to the Lord is to abandon oneself so completely that the disposal of affection is included in the act, and all now belongs to Him so entirely that it must be directed wheresoever He wills; it belongs to Him, unreservedly. Thus, if He designs to unite us to any soul (even if it differ completely from our own) without other sympathy but in the love of Christ, our part must be to follow the Divine Will as cheerfully as if we were to unite ourselves with God Himself; with joy even greater! In similar circumstances natural feelings and self-seeking might very probably detract from the merit of the action.

Natural imperfection may, perhaps, make us complain, but let us always remember that to give our heart to God means to give it also to all that is loved by God.

Thus the divine Word, Who, in His own essence is love, and can love only the Father, loves us also in that infinite love that unites the Father and the Son. Because Christ, merely considering in man the real and living likeness of the Divinity, loves man as He loves the Father. So, on our part, let us love Christ in our brethren, seeing in them Himself only.

And, just as Jesus Christ opens His Heart to all who long to penetrate It's secrets; so ought we, in all truth and simplicity be ready to open our poor hearts to all—allowing all to draw from thence affection and edification as they will, without trying to hide whatever might humiliate us in the eyes of others. Thus, our Lord Himself will be able to dispose of our hearts, and we shall love only Him, and our brethren in Him.

April 15, 1901

IV

When our love is but little enlightened, recollection suffers from our preoccupation with active work. If we allow this, we prefer some temporal thing before the peace of Christ, which is the only true Good and the Source of all that is good. But our recollection should give birth to our activity, which must draw from that all its fruitfulness, without ever entirely absorbing it.

May 19, 1901

V

Since Adam's fall, true joy is always the fruit of suffering, and finds its first cause in the suffering Hearts of Jesus and Mary. In proportion as the soul shares in these Sufferings does its joy become more or less deep.

Eternal bliss is the price of infinite suffering; of the outpouring of the Precious Blood which our Incarnate Lord drew from the Immaculate and Blessed Virgin Mary. The Mother gave It, in order that the Son might shed It, and thus she furnished the matter of the Sacrifice in such a way that the Son, immolating Himself, immolated the Mother too. The same Blood is shed, but the Sacrifice is double, for the Blood of the Son comes from the Heart of the Mother. Yes, to shed the one, is to break the other. The sword with one blow opened the Heart of the Son, and pierced the soul of the Mother. Their twofold Sacrifice gains heaven for us.

June 29, 1901

VI

Why did not the Evangelists open to souls the sanctuary of Love wherein the Hearts of Jesus and Mary are united and where, alone, were the virtues of Their dolourous Passion? It seems to be, because Jesus reserved for Himself to lead loving souls who are eager for solitude and suffering, into that Sanctuary.

July 9, 1901

Aspirations and Thoughts

VII

When the fire of love is once kindled in the soul, if it be carefully kept up and delicately tended, the tiny spark grows little by little, and gradually consumes everything that comes in its way. The flame develops, and by degrees takes complete possession of the soul, as if by its own action.

VIII

If a soul wishes to take due account of the Presence of God within itself, it should learn to live retired interiorly in complete silence and abandonment. Before long it will feel itself moved by a mysterious action which directs, supports and influences it, and from that time will understand how God dwells in it.

IX

Who would not admire and love the unalterable and sublime peace with which our Lady received alike the Divine Word into Her Bosom at the Incarnation, and received Him into Her arms, when taken down from the Cross on Calvary?

X

Our divine Lord gives Himself to us! not so much perhaps, that we should possess Him, as that He should possess us for our transformation into Him. We may contain His Humanity, but His Divinity contains us.

July 1901

XI

The union of souls is cemented in and by suffering. For our human nature, suffering is the soil where solid love grows; and to be united by suffering is a union of nature, because, since the Fall, suffering has penetrated our whole being. When a soul has disclosed the sufferings of its life, it has told all that can be said, and has revealed the inmost depths of itself.

July 25, 1901

XII

There is no complete union of the soul with Jesus without penetration into the secret mysteries of the Heart of the Divine Master. There it will find an ocean of love and an abyss of suffering. Such a vision as this produces the "holy folly of love"; it fills the heart of man with divine burnings, and wounds so deeply that the soul pours itself, once and forever, at the Feet of Him, Whom alone, henceforth it can love.

This, oh! my Master! this is the union to which Thou dost lead that soul who wishes sincerely to love and suffer with Thee.

XIII

In the work of Redemption, death is the beginning of life. Our Lady annihilated Herself in pronouncing Her "Fiat," and thence was the beginning of the Life of the Man-God. Her Son submitted to the death of the body and hence came the resurrection of souls. And in the exact degree that each of us dies to his own will, he is born again in the life of Grace.

XIV

A soul in love with the beauties of nature, which reveal God to it does not want to dissect in genders and species the One, Indivisible Object of its admiration, but prefers to contemplate the works of the Creator with the simplicity of love.

Is it not enough for the enthusiasm of a pure soul to admire the picturesque rocks in a lovely valley; to see their mantle of moss freshly watered drop by drop; the torrent rushing at their feet and then spreading a silver cloth over the verdant fields? A thousand flowerets perfume the air; hidden under its leaves, the violet is betrayed by its fragrance, the wild lilies open their chalices wide and look up to heaven. How many wonders of beauty that escape our notice!... And, if in the silence of your soul, you listen to that voice of nature that speaks to the heart, you will hear one flower telling you, "I speak of humility"—another—"I love purity."—the crystal water says, "I praise chastity"—and the rose calls aloud, "I sing of love."

Listen to all these voices chiming together in such wondrous harmony, and you will better understand the praise sent up by Nature to her Author.

XV

But... Must we repress our feelings as soon as they appear? Some people tell us that to cultivate them is to soften the soul—is to give to nature a certain empire over the supernatural, to expose the mind to submit to the incessant variations of the flesh, and to constrain it to abdicate in favour of a less noble faculty. Ought not the heart of a man to be tempered like steel, leaving tears and sentiment to women?... To feel is a weakness—to weep is cowardly, for sentiment is born of passion, and of that part of ourselves that the will ought to rule!... Indeed, it is so, my God! he who loves Thee by feelings only, does not love Thee fully...he seeks the sweetness of Thy love and does not love the rigour of Thy justice. But, to my mind, oh! Lord, the ardour of the soul should sanctify both the strength of the will and the refinement of feeling. My feelings come from Thee: it is only just that I should render them back to Thee again... Why should they be repudiated? If sentiment be rightly directed, it softens the heart without weakening it, and often delicately suggests more than the mind would have understood; it strengthens the soul in good, for it renders it supple to move and act for what is good.

Why, then, may we not be left to our joy in the presence of the beauties of nature? The work of Thy Hands, oh! Lord, is the manifestation of Thy loving-kindness; and our hearts cannot remain silent before Nature which chants aloud Thy love.

XVI

Almighty and all good God, when my soul gathers itself together in Thee; when, dazzled by the sight of Thine adorable Perfections revealed in everything that surrounds me, I close my eyes to exterior things and open wide the gaze of faith in the inner depths of my being, beholding there a Vision far more worthy of admiration, it is Thyself I contemplate there, oh! infinite Beauty! it is Thyself, oh! consuming Love! this it is that attracts and takes me captive with the cords of ineffable charity!

August 1901

XVII

Why is it, oh! Lord? Why is it that Thou urgest souls to attach themselves to Thee alone, and then, when they long to fly to Thee who callest them, Thou leavest them in their own impotence? Is not this a fresh sign of Thine unlimited love? Thou seemest to fetter our flight, which fancies it can attain to Thee, to teach us that we must depend entirely upon Thyself, and that, with Thy wings we shall fly more swiftly and surely.

XVIII

We need more experience of our own inconstancy, so as never again to depend upon human strength, but to lie still in Thine Arms which will carry us! And how sweet the perfect repose is of the loving soul in the Heart of the Divine Love!

XIX

Show me, oh! God—what in me most hinders Thine action. Teach me what are the imperfections and weaknesses that prevent me from losing myself in the abyss of Thy love by that interior union for which my soul yearns!

Why does not Thine infinite charity inflame the loving soul with the fire that at once purifies and consumes, instead of so often leaving it to its own efforts? Why dost Thou delay, and leave the soul to languish, separated from Thee, its Life-Giver? I do not know. But even now, what peace there is in that slumber which places us forever in the Divine Will, and gives us up to the power of love! The mind tries to dive into this mystery and wearies itself in the attempt, but love finds out its secrets—dwells in quiet and lies down in the confidence of self-abandonment in the Hands of its God.

XX

Man is born to love; his sole need is to love, to love. To love is his whole strength and his only joy. But to love *Thee*, oh! my God—this is the reason of his creation—this the need that presses him: *Thy Love!* He becomes strong in loving Thee: the calm rest he takes in Thee is all that gives him real joy—and so, man never ceases to seek for Thee until he finds himself lost in Thee forever, oh! uncreated Love!

XXI

Just as, in the depths of a severe winter, when the earth is frozen hard and the rivers ice-bound, the sun may rise and shine brightly and pour forth torrents of dazzling light but its rays cannot soften the land; so it is with a soul that contemplates the splendours of Eternal Truth without drawing near enough to the Sun of Justice to feel His life-giving warmth. Such a soul only seems to be alive. Light, alone, cannot arouse it from its heavy, death-like sleep.

On the other hand, a soul warmed and melted by the Divine Sun, has the heat of life remaining in it, although at the close of its day, shadows may draw around it, making it enter into chill darkness, as of death. It lives, even though it may seem dead—the warmth of life is still in it; sooner or later a brighter day will dawn, flooding the soul with its light and urging it on with unquenchable ardours.

August 5, 1901

XXII

To dwell within one's soul is to have heaven on earth, and he who knows how to do this, becomes the intimate companion of Jesus and contemplates the Blessed Trinity assiduously.

XXIII

When we feel that we are loved by someone, either we love him in return, or we soon learn to do so. And thus it is that Jesus-Christ conquers our souls. Oh! my sweetest Saviour! why should I resist Thy loving action? Grant me to feel Thy love, so that I may love Thee in return.

XXIV

The following lines were sent to L…on his ordination to the priesthood. I wanted to give him some little remembrance, and did not know what would be most suitable.…Eventually I gave him nothing but sent the following "Thoughts."

The mutability of human things is so great that we seek in vain for a secure foothold. The world would fain arrest our minds carried away by the impetuous flood, and gives some token of remembrance. The true monk, however, lets the torrent rush on, and only asks of God, to hold his mind firmly fixed on Him—and on Him to anchor his soul.

Thus it seems to me needless to offer you anything as a "Memento." Besides—how can I give you aught else but love, since all our wealth consists in the one fact that we belong entirely to God? He is the Master, and has accepted our *all*, giving it back to us in Himself. So do I give you myself—lost in God—and only wish to make you know the depths of my soul and the love with which I long to see you inflamed.

Why should we want any material remembrance to fix in our memories the deed of this ordination day, when, every day, its memorial will sink more deeply into our souls? For ordination is, as it were a print which will be more deeply impressed into our souls every day we live. It is the seal of divine love—for the priest is *another Christ*, and Christ is love. Love is the cause of the priest; therefore, to love more is to become a better priest.

Why is it, oh! my God, that the mind so often withdraws itself from Thee, and that the blind heart attaches itself to things of no worth? Would it satisfy the heart of man to follow, "ever without rest," the rush of the tide of daily events, and to allow passing things to absorb his soul?

No, indeed, man yearns for Eternity. He who stays to linger over passing vanities, touches, but cannot elevate them, and hardly deceives himself as to their absolute worthlessness. The mind can never be satisfied until it attain to God, the Infinite. It lowers itself by stooping to finite attractions. This is not to love, but to stifle love; and here is the supreme suicide. The heart may succumb to this abasement, but it will for a long time have been turning towards God, and aspiring after His love!

Thou teachest our souls to love Thee, my God. Thou wouldest possess them wholly and utterly. Behold them here, oh! Master; search and see if there be yet any fibre in them that does not tend to Thee. Give Thyself to our souls, in order that they may belong entirely to Thee. Why dost Thou so enthral our hearts, forcing them to love Thee, if then Thou wilt hide Thyself and leave us to our own weakness? us! poor children who, alone, can only totter! Yet even here, is there not a fresh proof of Thy love?

Thy priests have received Thine anointing, oh! Lord, and are annihilated in their own sight. They are vested and girt with Thy strength and, their own weakness appalls them. This is because Thy holy unction must be their only power and Thine Arm their only strength. It is thus, indeed, that their souls ought to rest in Thee.

Yes; divine love is a holy madness. Our souls are passionately in love with Thee, Lord Jesus! Thy gifts conquer us—Thy tenderness inspires us. Oh! what can we give in return to Him Who today grants to you to go up to His Altar, and to me the joy of seeing and sharing in your happiness?

August 12, 1901

XV

How sweet it is to suffer, and how delightful is the solitude of the Cross! These joys are understood only by those who know what it is to love. It seems to me that just as the fall of night brings welcome rest in sleep to a strong and healthy man, whilst to an invalid it means hours of increased weariness, so, a soul that is strengthened by love finds its very rest in suffering, but a feeble soul finds bitterness and loss of peace.

Suffering isolates from creatures. He who knows God is drawn into closer union with Him by suffering, but he who knows Him not, loses everything—created things fall away from him, and to divine things he is a stranger.

To unite oneself to Thee, my God, in the silence of crucified nature, of a humble spirit, with a pure heart and in oblivion of all besides—this is not merely to love—but to live!

Suffering consoles; death repays.

XXVI

A poor man in need, does not go to another poor man—but to one who is rich. And just in the same way the soul, which, isolated by suffering, should turn to man for comfort in its distress, will gain little or nothing from him, and will not find God. But let him only lift up his eyes and the Lord will come and give himself to that soul: here we see the value of suffering and how it is rewarded by divine consolation.

XXVII

When twilight is ended and all around is silent, and nature alone, plunged in profound recollection, speaks aloud of the Divine Author of all things: then the pure soul hears and understands Thee, oh! God. But the sinner trembles and fears to hear Thy Voice.

Yes, indeed—at the close of an autumn day, some mysterious influence which I cannot express seems to descend from heaven, and to hush the noises of broad day, even as the fading of noontide glare. How good it is—this time of peaceful dusk, enwrapping our very being and penetrating us with the sense of our need of love! So, surely, when all is tranquilly silent within the soul, when the passions seem to sleep and cease to excite it to the feverish pursuit of frivolous things, or even to a restless search after things divine—if the soul know how to dwell "at home within itself"—what loving silence it will find in this interior sanctuary

This solitude is full of God!

September 1901

XXVIII

Banish all haste from your actions, for it destroys recollection and hinders love.

To be recollected is to love, and when love acts, it always does so swiftly.

October 12, 1901

XXIX

Love carries us away, where it attracts us, and one who loves God is drawn towards Heaven unawares, and this is prayer. Consequently, to love much is to pray much to love always—or to live by love—is, therefore, to, pray always and never tire.

October 13, 1901

XXX

We love others because we are sharers in the same nature: the closer this participation, the greater love we mutually owe.[74]

XXXI

A nature that could be hateful to itself would be a monstrosity. We necessarily love ourselves, but this self-love may be of a kind that encroaches on the love we owe to our neighbour; and it is called *egotism*. There is another kind of love which is born of the love of God, and is the principle of our love of others. This is really *charity*, which alone knows how to be self-sacrificing.

XXXII

As you have received much, give freely. Be merciful to others with a generosity like to that which comes from heaven. To fail in this point would restrain the divine indulgence within yourself.

---

[74] Here the question regards the *divine nature*, in which we are sharers by grace; all men do not possess this in the same degree. So we may say that we do not all possess the perfection of human nature in an equal measure: and that, in this sense, the more human we are, so much the more are we worthy of esteem and of love.

XXXIII

Love warms and enlightens: he who begins to love soon learns the meanness of his own love and the need for greater purity of heart. He had thought himself worthy to please the Lord, and now finds that he is the object of immeasurable indulgence.

October 25, 1901

XXXIV

Labour is preceded and followed by rest; rest restores the strength and fits it for fresh effort.

So it ought to be with the soul of the monk. *His* work is divine praise; his rest is prayer. In the first, he sings to God; in the second, he reposes in Him; first celebrating the Object of its love, and then giving itself up to the caresses of that Love Whom it adores. In that solemn prayer, the soul like a soaring eagle gives a few strokes with its wings, but soon rests in prayer and lets itself be borne on the impetus of grace.

XXXV

Sacrifice is only costly when love is imperfect. To be devoted to God, means sacrifice. Thou, oh! God, knowest how happy a loving soul is that has devoted itself absolutely to Thee, and feels itself entirely Thine own! To sacrifice oneself is to forget oneself in order to remember God alone: this is the true life of the soul; this is unmixed happiness; this is heaven on earth.

XXXVI

True friendship is a blossom fragrant with the good odour of Christ. A heart that is capable of appreciating the refinements of friendship, feels the need of possessing another heart that will return the sweetness of their mutual perfume. If heaven should withhold from it such another loving heart, it must stand on its guard lest this noble gift should be stifled within itself, in order to escape from its loneliness. Let that heart look up to heaven, even though the heavens seem as brass. There is to be found the only reason for the refusal. Jesus Himself wants that heart, for His own friend.

XXXVII

When we believe that we have really given Thee our all and seek vainly for anything more to offer Thee; when Thy Charity has melted away the ice of our self-love, and the chillness of preoccupation from our hearts, when we fancy we have done all in our power, or, at least have neglected nothing to gain Thy love; then it is shown us that we are really only beginning to love! Charity is God's work. Perhaps we have done our part; perhaps God's hour draws near. We may implore His help, but, of ourselves, we cannot produce its effects. Charity only flourishes in the soul at the delicate touch of the Spirit. The soul must await the life-giving breath of Divine Love.

Oh! my God—is it not yet time to touch my heart and to light the flame of love in it?—for I do not know what more to offer Thee and I feel that; yet I scarcely even love Thee!

XXXVIII

If we really love, and find the portrait of our God insulted in any way, our heart bleeds and we long to make amends anyhow for the offence. We kiss the picture with respect and love, grieving that vile creatures in their pride have made it an object of scorn and contempt: we wash off its stains, and try by every means in our power to remove the slightest trace of the profane sacrilege. And it is just the same with those who love souls. Each soul is an image of God, a likeness too often defiled by sin.

Thinking of this, if we meet a soul that has fallen into sin it makes our heart ache and we are indignant at the behaviour of the cruel and hypocritical world. But this is not enough for a fervent lover of God. He draws near and respectfully kisses the poor sinner, recognizing in him the image of God, and he takes every pains to lead the stripped wanderer back again to his true Good. Love is not satisfied with uttering words of comfort; love must act; it offers itself as a victim of reparation; it takes on itself the crimes of sinners, and, as far as possible, pays the debt to Divine Justice.

Working for souls means helping them; first by praying for them, but most of all by suffering. The direction of souls supposes, in the Shepherd, first austerity and suffering in his own person, compassion and kindness for his flock.

October 11, 1901

XXXIX.

Oh! Jesus! Thou hast taught me to thirst after Thee! I entreat Thee to quench this thirst, which is my soul's only desire. Thou hast implanted in me this hunger and this thirst after Thy divine Love—but when, oh! Lord, wilt Thou satisfy my yearning heart?

XL

There is a great difference between giving oneself up to love, or to friendship.

We must love everyone, but friendship limits itself generally to certain souls destined by God for our comfort.

Love unites by drawing together; friendship blends by uniting. Union by love is deep, but, may exist with a certain separation: friendship supposes a familiar and habitual intercourse. As long as friendship is true, God is its Seal, its Strength and its Guardian. This bond can only exist between souls whose love is as a furnace, as pure as crystal and as chaste as a flame.

December 15, 1901

XLI

When the soul begins to love, it rises up towards God: and when it loves more (when its love increases) it flows out to its neighbour in whom it finds God. Thus imitating Jesus in His love for souls.

But to work for souls through love means suffering. Yes, the labour of suffering is the labour of love. It is true, Christ died for all, and, in His Sufferings all men possess inexhaustible treasure; but still it is by our own sufferings that we gain access to that Treasure.

To suffer for souls is to draw near to the Fountain of life for them, and to make the riches of Christ flow out over them.

December 21, 1901

XLII

It seems easier to relieve Christ in the person of others, than in our own selves. The mists of evil hide Jesus, there where we ought to find Him first. We often see charitable persons who *give* generously, but who have not enough virtue to *receive* with simplicity.

XLIII

The more deeply seated the evil, the more patience is needed to root it out; and the hardened sinner can only be vanquished by the charity of a soul that is unwearied and is willing to wait.

A painful wound requires a hand at once firm and delicate, which, whilst working energetically against the malady, treats it with increasing gentleness as it goes deeper and deeper, and becomes more keenly painful. The sinner's wounds, far from repelling a soul that is truly charitable, bring out brightly its devotedness and delicacy; its compassion increases with the suffering, and this is the secret of the miracles worked on souls.

We go near a fire to warm ourselves and if the cold increases we get the bellows and blow up the flame. Just in the same way, when a soul is frozen up by sin, let us warm it by contact with the love that is burning in our own soul in its regard: if the cold resists it and perhaps increases, let us blow up the flame of charity in ourselves, and seek by every means in our power to communicate fresh warmth of love to that poor soul well-nigh dead with cold.

December 25, 1901

XLIV

The soul is a dwelling that must be inhabited; a nuptial chamber where it unites itself to its Beloved. Since the heart of man can find no rest but in God, the Lord alone by right can enter there. This is its title to the name of a sanctuary. It is the solitude where man meets with his God, and learns to know and to love Him.

None can enter there, none can cross the threshold of that sanctuary unless he has been admitted. At the entrance a guardian angel stands, who is free to admit and powerful to expel. That Guardian is Love. Love is stronger than death. Even God Himself respects the opposition which He too often meets. He waits patiently, however, and His longsuffering mercy knocks again and again and again. But if He meet with refusal until the appointed hour of Justice, He will withdraw,—and forever! Then His absence will leave a void, the torture of which will exceed any other pain that the soul can endure.

Thus, the soul is a holy, an inviolable dwelling. There are some who open their dwelling wide, to admit spirits of darkness, by giving it up to sin: these drive out the holy Spirit of God, and prefer hate to love.

There are others, who draw back from opening their heart to God because the austerity of chaste love frightens them, and they do not know the charms of the divine solitude of the soul.... These are the children of this world, whose eyes are darkened by frivolity, and whose tepidity drives their only Good away.

Finally, there are those who open their whole soul to God, and who possess Him, to live with Him there forever, knowing Him and loving Him. It is only these last, who understand that the soul is a dwelling indeed.

XLV

What does *surrendering the soul* imply? It means the opening of that inviolable sanctuary to some one—and allowing him free right of entry as he wills, there to consummate and perfect union.

When the freedom of that city is given to any creature, it is a very serious thing.

But fearlessly open your soul to Jesus! Look up, like the field lilies to heaven, and open out wide. The divine dew will come down upon you—giving you life; that is to say the love, the charity, that purifies and unites the soul with God.

December 29, 1901

XLVI

Jacob loved Rachel, and served Laban seven years that she might be his…and so the soul labours and toils during the whole of its life to gain possession of Jesus. But to live without Him or to work without Him for only one year would be too heavy a burden for its weak love. Mercy, therefore, must come to the rescue and impose some easier conditions on its feebleness. Jesus Himself comes, and in His company the soul works lovingly, being set on fire by that Love that "many waters cannot quench."

XLVII

Ah! my God! how the soul seeks to know Thee! But all that it knows is too little to assuage the thirst that devours it, and all that it knows *not* is too vast a field for it to explore!

The impenetrable secrets of Nature and the divine mysteries are such as to hold it stupified before them, the truth which it cannot penetrate. But one thing remains, and when this is truly understood, it is sufficient for all. This lies in the fact that *to know* is not everything; knowledge is but the way leading to love.

If the soul has realised that it cannot peer into Thee because the brightness of Thy Face dazzles its feeble intelligence—if experience has taught it to be satisfied with the dark light of *faith* only, in penetrating Thy mysteries, then, for the future it grasps the fact that one may know little yet love greatly.

XLVIII

The bridegroom does not know his bride until he leads her into the bridal chamber: neither does a friend know his friend until he comes, intimately, into his home.

"Why then?" cries the soul, "why then, oh! my tender Master, am I Thy spouse and have promised fidelity to Thee, and yet have not been able to gain entrance into Thy Sacred Heart? Why dost Thou take me as Thy friend, and yet I am kept out from the divine home of Thy Heart?"

Do not answer that I am but too unworthy to be Thy little spouse! On my own authority I would not have dared to presume to such Espousals! But since, oh! Lord, Thy folly was so great as to love my soul, why dost Thou not purify and admit me to union with Thee?

December 30, 1901

1902

XLIX

For long, man lived under the law of the flesh: but now, by grace he lives according to the Spirit, and has exchanged the abjection of a fallen nature for the dignity of a deified nature.

The fleshly nature remains, but is supernaturalised. We must then distinguish what is human from what is divine, following grace only and being contented to make use of nature subordinately and to see by Faith enlightening reason. This is the secret of true greatness. Man walks by the feeble light as of a torch—that is to say, the light of *reason*: the Sun of Truth rises, and then he is in future illuminated by cloudless day.

January 3, 1902

L

Hearts and minds that are not narrow never find reasons to be scandalised. The only just motive for taking scandal would be to see Truth err, or to see Good do evil; and this can never be.

Many certainly think they see it happen, but this is because they see so little or so dimly that they confuse the spirit with the letter, nature with grace. This is why people of limited intelligence and cowardly souls are easily scandalised.

LI

To love a pure soul is in itself a purification of love. Sometimes a soul that approaches another from human motives, does not find what it was seeking, but finds, instead, a nature that has been transformed by contact with the divine; and to meet with such a soul often has the effect of attracting to sincere love of God.

January 4, 1902

LII

In order to love everyone, begin by loving God, and all else in Him: see the Incarnate God everywhere and in all things; and in the Virgin's Son recognise and love the Son of the Most High. Love in the Church the Spouse of Christ: but here distinguish between the human and the divine; between nature and grace. You will always find both, and thus, consequently, you will always find something to be loved, and something to be excused.

January 9, 1902

LIII

According as a man directs his life—whether towards God or towards his own self, so will he either expand in love, or diminish and shrink in egotism.

The one important thing, therefore, is to love God above everything else, in such a way that love is the spring of all our actions and that our whole life may be kindled with divine charity.

Love may be gauged by the fulness with which it gives. Let us, then, give ourselves entirely to God: our bodily strength, the energy of our will, our powers of mind and imagination. With regard to our neighbour we should act in the same way, by entirely devoting our strength to his needs, if circumstances should ask it: showering on him the sweetness and warmth of love and gently warming his soul by delicate, soothing touches. In short, we must put all the powers of our mind at his service, whether by sharing our thoughts with him, or, above all, by encouraging him to pour out his own easily, for everyone likes to have his thoughts and ideas understood and appreciated.

Here is perfect love and the full gift of self. This donation, when made to God with humility and to our neighbour with sweetness, produces holiness and fills the soul with the life of God.

January 10, 1902

LIV

To give your strength and love to your neighbour is a good work; but he will never meet you with both hands unless he finds in you a mind ready to hear his views and large enough to enter into them.

Your mind seems always in a sort of stronghold, an entrenched camp, ready to judge and dominate everything. The ideas of others only find a welcome insofar as they fall in with your own; beyond that limit, they are condemned either to give way or to see themselves repelled without pity. Oh! this will never do. This is intellectual pride which thinks it knows everything, and does not even perceive the mist of ignorance which enshrouds it on every hand!

LV

Consider the greatness of "Thought" in man.[75] It is his ideal. Every soul that wants to grow has an ideal—only one—up to which he works. For this "Thought" is a mysterious force which gives unity to existence, directing, animating and giving value to all life.

It is by means of this light that the soul forms its conception of all things. Its "Thought" is for it the measure of all perfection.

The leading thought, or ideal of a Christian is that part of His Truth which God marks out for his study and his love; it points out the part which God means him to play in the world.

To understand the *thought* of a soul, then, is to know it perfectly, to measure the greatness of its love. From this we see the great respect we must have for the *thoughts* of others.

---

[75] "THOUGHT" here means, the *ideal* which directs the whole life.

Aspirations and Thoughts

LVI

In loving the souls of others it is not so much that we find in them our own manner of thinking and acting, nor only—in an abstract way—because we see Jesus-Christ dwelling in them.

We must greatly esteem and love in each soul its own way of being and thinking; for this is often the special form under which Christ dwells in that soul. Let us then admit into our own minds the *thoughts* of our neighbour; so that we love him more intimately and tenderly. This, in a way is to open our mind to admit Jesus-Christ there under a particular form, as, by Faith, we receive God wholly.

January 11, 1902

LVII

My heart suffers from two causes; having to restrain affection, and having to bear with small-minded people's distortion, of our most unintentional actions, thinking they show too particular friendship. For such pains there is no other remedy than the love of Christ. It enlarges and divinely ennobles the soul; raising it above the littlenesses of earthly life, it fills the soul with compassion for those who are shrivelled by the meanness of the world, and teaches it to love without stint and without ever growing weary. For everywhere and in all it is God and for God that we love.

January 12, 1902

LVIII

Incompetent and complaisant admirers of those whom they believe to be saints, may very justly be said to be like those who, always living in towns, gush about the beauties of nature.

Listen to those fine poets describing fields enamelled with flowers, bathed by limpid rivulets, or depicting the majestic trees of a forest, and you feel at once that these chatterers have never heard the great voice of nature. They have never seen the immense and glorious beauties, never drank in the sweet perfume of the mists, nor have they probed nor understood the deep secrets of Creation. In their descriptions will generally be found merely the fruits of a lively imagination and superficial feelings. Those people, wide awake to the things of the world neither know nor care that nature has been created by Supreme Love for the purpose of chanting the praise of its Divine Author.

Thus, many who notice a very feeble ray from the Sun of Justice shining in a soul, or feel some little effect of warmth emanating from that soul (though it may be very cold, really), imagine they see a brilliant star, and think they draw near to a burning furnace! And yet it is really a mere nothing—perhaps but enough to show how weak it is, and how dully it burns!

LIX

To live by God, is to possess a soul raised so high above earthly things that it finds itself a stranger to all that does not speak of Divine Love in some way or other.

LX

The really strong soul always acts with extreme sweetness of love.

Prayer springs from the heart as water flows from its source. Both gush out easily and abundantly; both are crystal-clear; for the one flows from a rock, the other from the Rock that is Christ. Both pour out peacefully, one into the calm of the great woods—the other in the Solitude of the Heart of Jesus. The natural source dries up sometimes, whilst the soul that knows how to pray is ever fruitful because she draws ever freshly from the Fount of Life, which springs up even for all Eternity.

January 15, 1902

LXI

A really valuable book, and a direction wisely given derive their inspiration from mature thought. If the reading of the book let you into the author's thought, or if you follow the directions given with the intelligence required, you can rest assured that you have read well and obeyed well. After that, you need not burden your memory with details as to the number or disposition of the paragraphs of the book, since you have taken in its teaching: neither should you worry yourself as to the formulary of the order given you. Be satisfied with having executed it well.

January 20, 1902

LXII

A good action, being not so much the work of human frailty as of the divine Mercy, is not our best claim to merit before God. Man has his little share—not much more than his goodwill—the great part is God's, since it was He Who inspired the thought and gave the strength to perform the action. Thus, such an act is at once a sign and an assured pledge of God's goodness in our regard. Our true Title to the Divine favour is the Blood of Christ, to which we have the right through our own destitution and humbly acknowledged frailty.

January 26, 1902

LXIII

Moral disorder results from a want of patience. To give in to temptation, to fly in the midst of difficulties, is to lose patience. In order to fight efficaciously against this evil and come off the victor, we must "possess our soul in patience": according to the precept of Christ.

LXIV

When man has come to his full strength he enjoys his prime but a short while; death has already begun its work of destruction.

February 15, 1902

LXV

A pure kiss is the great mark of love. A kiss may be given from different motives, as there are many kinds of love—but it is always the sign of a perfect union, of mutual and entire complacency.

An obedient and submissive son has the right to kiss his father. Misconduct or disobedience deprive him of that right.

Brotherly devotion, faithful friendship, sympathetic charity may all be indicated by a kiss. But if any offence or coldness had diminished the warmth of these feelings, the sign would be false.

A true, sincere and faithful kiss is a noble act; but a false kiss is an infidelity, and almost always a betrayal. This mark of affection should only be given between persons united by blood or marriage. Between friends it should have only the meaning of union of souls; sensual motives should have no part there. The kiss of friendship is so great and noble a sign that it is given around the Altar. Here it is the christian kiss, and under these conditions remains pure and sublime as love itself. But who knows the worth of a kiss? On all sides, this sign—like love itself—is profaned.

February 23, 1902

LXVI

In order to live a life of recollection and prayer by oneself, solid virtue is required; but greater virtue is needed for a life of active charity. This supposes a profound humility, making us see in all others the good we see not in our own selves; a simplicity which interprets everything favourably, even excusing evil when possible.

February 25, 1902

LXVII

It is never according to good manners to show disdain for another's opinion, nor to raise one's voice imperiously; but for a *young* man to do so is particularly out of place. Assurance and decision in expressing one's views belong to those whose age gives them mature experience and in younger persons is generally a consequence of ignorance; they have only seen and known very little—at the most but one side of a question, and persuade themselves very quickly and generally sincerely that there can be no other view. For them, everything is obvious and certain.

When the mind has been enriched with more knowledge and experience slowly acquired during many years: then, indeed it seems that certainty might be arrived at on solid foundations. But, even so, a learned and prudent man scarcely ever lays down the law; or, if he should do so, it would be with great caution. Such a man is sure to speak modestly, diffidently, because experience will have taught him that (beyond the regions of Faith) there are very few *certainties*.

February 28, 1902

LXVIII

Oh! God, grant me the strength to be gentle, and enough calmness to be strong. Grant me Thy love, which will make me stronger than death, so that, with this love I may possess that mildness at whose touch difficulties easily give way.

March 4, 1902

LXIX

When divine love has grown sufficiently in the soul to produce union between the soul and God; when that union has become deep enough to bear no longer the fragile stamp of human fidelity, but depends solely on the strong foundations of Faith in immutable Truth; when that union has gained enough intimacy to allow of a holy familiarity (born of a more enlightened knowledge of the Divinity)—then, for the first time, the soul sees itself in God. The sight of the Infinite teaches it the nothingness of the finite: as soon as the soul considers the Divine Goodness, immediately it sees its own wretchedness. The warmth of divine Charity makes it feel the chill of its own tepidity. The Vision of the great *All* produces the understanding and scorn of the *Nothing*. It ponders over these things with the strength of reason and now it fathoms them by the light of Faith. Formerly its action was guided by human wisdom, but henceforward by the touch of a divine influence. The soul now feels its own very littleness but this gives it an infinite peace, for even its own nothingness is to it a divine truth, divinely understood.

LXX

We ought to love enough to act—not by the thought of painful duty, but by the demands of love…and this, everywhere and in all things.

LXXI

Many things come into the human heart; many feelings have their birth there; and, in all this, one only thing has the right, even at times the duty, and more often, the need to pour itself out. *This is Divine Love.*

LXXII

One who by nature is affectionate and tender, often suffers at feeling himself held back by a timid and reserved exterior, which keeps aloof the hearts of those whom he would divinely attract: he longs to pour out the ardours of holy love for them.

March 7, 1902

Aspirations and Thoughts

LXXIII

To give ourself up to divine love spells suffering, abandonment to suffering; for the furnaces of love are abysses of suffering.

But the world, incapable of understanding God's designs on the suffering of pure and generous souls, says lightly that this poisons happy lives.

Nevertheless it must be granted that sorrow, to a Christian (like salt in the ocean) is the healthy element that purifies and preserves.

LXXIV

The world will not find any fault with you for falling in love with a creature; that is the order of nature. But if, in all simplicity you reveal the warmth of your feelings towards God, you will be taxed with exaggeration, and silenced at once. And yet, is not the rule and perfection of all true love there? Why will they not let us say "I love God supremely," when not one of them would find fault with us for expressing love for a creature?—and that, even in such excessive terms as "I adore the girl"—"I am head over heels in love with that man!"

April 10, 1902

LXXV

When a man has succeeded in any enterprise, he congratulates himself on having produced what is worthy of him; and, pleased with his work, he forgets that every production is sure to betray the faults of the mind that conceived it.

It is always wise to submit what you think you have done well, to the judgement of others: brighter minds than your own will add lustre to your work, and the work will gain by this.

LXXVI

Perfect knowledge and a just appreciation of things show us the Truths of Faith as realities far more substantial than any in the material order.

April 14, 1902

LXXVII

A grace of detachment does not only bring with it the strength to leave aside the special object to which the heart attaches itself at the expense of divine love; it gives also light to show the triviality of the object. We may feel all the difficulty the separation entailed, but this comes from the breaking of the fetter which was hindering the free flight of the soul.

April 19, 1902

LXXVIII

When the loving soul feels its own nothingness, it is flooded by an immense joy and unfailing peace. God may hide Himself and make the loving soul suffer in consequence, but the soul, knowing well its own worthlessness, goes on rejoicing in the profound happiness of being one of His creatures.

May 2, 1902

LXXIX

This morning before the Office, dawn had just begun, the clearness of the sky and freshness of the air foretold a warm and brilliant day, and by the time we had finished singing Lauds, the sun had risen like a globe of fire above the horizon. Its brilliance had not become so fierce but that the eye could rest on its calm light: a single glance could take in its whole subdued disk at once. However, a few hours later it had risen high in the blue sky and from those unspanned heights it was flooding the earth with dazzling light and fiery rays.

The thought came to me, that pure souls are like that. Some of them begin life as a radiant dawn, and many signs foretell that it will be a beautiful day. The Divine Sun of Justice rises on these lovely souls, as in a pure and deep empyrean. His course there is rapid, for nothing checks it, nor does anything cloud its growing brilliancy. At the fulness of day, it burns in these souls with so bright a light that it even dazzles them, although they are so privileged, and the object of so many favours.

LXXX

A loveless nature is like a sunless spring. The flowers may unfold but they have no charm: the fruits may ripen, but they have no flavour.

May 15, 1902

LXXXI

The death of a God, dying for the salvation of men, is a central point in the history of mankind. All ages bear witness to and converge towards it: the preceding centuries point to its coming: the others are destined to harvest its fruits.

The death of Christ is the centre of history, and also the centre of the life of each man in particular. In the Eyes of God every man will be great in proportion as he takes part in that Deed; for the only true and eternal dignity is that belonging to the Divine Priest. The degree of each one's holiness will be in exact proportion as he participates in that bloody immolation, For the Lamb of God alone is holy.

But although Jesus-Christ the divine High Priest appeared only once on earth, to offer up His Great Sacrifice on Calvary; yet, every day He appears in the person of each one of His ministers, to renew His Sacrifice on the Altar. In every altar, then, Calvary is seen: every altar becomes an august place, the Holy of holies, the Source of all holiness. Thither all must go to seek Life, and thither all must continually return, as to the source of God's mercies. Those who are the Master's privileged ones, never leave this holy place, but there they "find a dwelling," near to the altar, so that they never need go far from it; such are monks, whose first care it is to raise temples worthy to contain altars. Making their home by the Sanctuary, they consecrate their life to the divine worship, and every day sees them grouped around the Altar for the holy Sacrifice. This is the Event of the day, the centre to which the Hours, like the centuries, all converge: some as Hours of preparation and awaiting in the recollection of the Divine Praise—these begin with Lauds and Prime continued by Terce, the third Hour of the day: the others, Sext, None, Vespers and Compline, flow on in the joys of thanksgiving until sunset when the monks chant the closing in of night.

Thus the days of life pass, at the foot of the Altar; thus the life of man finds its greatness and its holiness in flowing out, so to say, upon the Altar, there to mingle with that Precious Blood which is daily shed in that hallowed place: for, if the life of man is as a valueless drop of water, when lost in the Blood of Christ it acquires an infinite value and can merit the divine mercy for us. He who knows what the Altar is, from it learns to live: to live by the Altar is to be holy, pleasing to God,— and to go up to the altar to perform the sacred Mysteries is to be clothed with the most sublime of all dignities after that of the Son of God and His holy Mother.[76]

May 19, 1902

LXXXII

When Love has once been given entrance into a generous soul, it demands *all*—one thing after another until it is drained of all that

---

[76] Alluding to the ceremony at the Offertory of the Mass where the priest mixes a drop of water with the wine.

is of self. The soul then feels its own absolute powerlessness, but it begins to feel also its strength in God.

Oh! God—how Thou hast drained my poor soul! And now, what dost Thou ask further? Give to it something that it can offer back to Thee! It belongs utterly to Thee because it has renounced even the possession of Thyself, its only Love—it has renounced possessing Thee a moment sooner than Thine infinite Wisdom has decreed.

June 3, 1902

LXXXIII

The most trying persons are often those who know least how much strength is needed to bear with them.

June 3, 1902

LXXXIV

It seems to me that the life of a holy soul flows as naturally towards suffering as the river flows to the sea: such a soul walks towards Christ, and Christ is, for man, ever a "hidden God," suffering and annihilated.

LXXXV

Jesus-Christ is the great Master of souls. He nourishes them with His Flesh, His Blood and His whole Self. He really makes Himself their Food. And, just so, it seems to me that no one receives the care of souls without taking upon himself the duty of feeding them with his own self. We must give ourselves up to the souls put in our charge, with such fullness of love that the grace given to our own souls shall overflow into theirs.

We shall meet, perhaps, with souls that are famished, weak or wounded: little souls that throw themselves on to us, and would fain feed from us with too great avidity and familiarity. Such conduct will wound us, as it wounds Jesus-Christ. But after His Example we must feed these poor sheep, in order that they may recover strength and life.

Oh! Jesus, from this day forward grant that the souls given into my care may draw from my poor heart the grace that Thou givest me. It is Thou, Thyself Who hungerest; eat, then, and drink all that Thou findest in my poor house. May my soul be a manger where Thy lambs can be filled with Thee.

June 4, 1902

LXXXVI

A priest who is penetrated with the spirit of his priesthood, is a man of sorrows. He bears the burden of other souls, their troubles, faults and needs. To become a priest is to be chosen by the Holy Ghost to follow Christ in His agony in the garden, to rise up with the Divine Master and to climb in His Steps, up the Mount of Calvary.

When, then, one has taken the first steps in the Sanctuary, which open the holy way to the Priesthood, that divine vocation more often brings the vision of suffering to the terrified soul, than of honour.

But the fervent soul accepts this dolorous ministry, which even beforehand makes it share in some way in the immolation of the Cross.

July 27, 1902

LXXXVI

My soul clamours for the liberty of a bird that has the freedom of the sky. It passes from one land to another and always lives like a king in the blue air of the firmament. Just so, the soul that has taken flight towards its God, finds in Him the immensity of the Infinite: it soars above the events of life and sees them passing, without, itself, leaving the upper regions of the Divine.

If sometimes it descends to earth for a moment it is but to attract by its chant of love other souls who have been captivated by the illusions of earth and become forgetful of the charms of heaven. That soul longs to free them from the mire of the world, to draw them upward in its own wake, and raise them above all that passes here below. Then God's little bird takes up again its free flight and its joyous course. It stops, just when love suggests, but never gives up its precious liberty of *flying in God* without let or hindrance, and of leaving the earth and even souls if they wished to keep it down: for the creature cannot hinder love for the Creator.[77]

LXXXVIII

The true Christian lives by that love which accepts all the happenings that God sends—adapts himself to them and directs them all to Him. The worldling chooses and prepares events, hunts after and adapts them to himself according to his taste, to live by and revel in them according to his fancy, so as to make up his own life of these, and fritter it away.

July 1902

LXXXIX

Prayer is the lifting of the soul to God: and a very close and simple union of the soul with its divine Master supposes, on its own side, that desirable state wherein it lives always in an atmosphere of prayer.

XC

Suffering is to a holy soul like burning liquid poured over a wound. It spreads all over it, slowly it soaks into the living flesh, causing acute pain: but the grievousness of the remedy is often the promise of a cure.

---

[77] Having met with inordinate sympathy from a certain person, Dom Pius here asserts his freedom of affection.

Then—oh, courageous soul! let suffering sink into the inmost depths of thy heart; drink this life-giving liquid; do not waste a single drop! And, if suffering sometimes quite overfloods thy soul and thou hast been able to assimilate it with the generous patience that keeps the heart in calmness and peace,—thou wilt have learned how sweet it is to suffer. For the bitterness of suffering changes into mysterious delight only at the precise moment when the soul has drained it to the dregs.

July 30, 1902

XCI

The soul that is in faithful friendship with Christ is like a beautiful, fragrant flower. Both the soul and the flower, planted in fertile soil, draw thence the food suited to their nature: they delight all who come near to them by their sweet perfume; their lovely appearance demands admiration—for, whoever looks at such as these, contemplates God, and loves Him more.

But, if any bold hand should snatch one of these beautiful flowers, it would wither, its beauty would fade away and its sweet odour disappear: for the works of God cannot bear the coarse touch of man.

August 1, 1902

Aspirations and Thoughts

1903

XCII

I feel that, sometimes, the thorns and lance of suffering open a bleeding wound in the soul; but to a Christian, this wound is at once painful and consoling, for it is the door that Jesus Christ opens in order to enter further into His home, there to light the fire of His love. When once the soul understands this, it is careful not to avoid these painful pricks, but, on the contrary, it lets them transpierce it through and through.

XCIII

An irritable soul takes up arms at the least offence, and often at merely a slight rudeness: holding itself on the defensive, it is ready to return blow for blow, to wound as it has been wounded, and to hurl pointed darts. If these hit their aim, the soul perfidiously rejoices.

But the disciple of Christ acts quite otherwise. He remains peaceful. Injuries hurt him; he receives them, but he never retaliates; he offers to his enemy a heart that does not weary of being ill-treated, but remains open, notwithstanding everything; ever ready to receive and welcome its brother with love and sweetness.

February 7, 1903

XCIV

If we go into a forest for a cool rest, we choose a solitary place sheltered by tall, shady trees, where there is grass and soft moss, and sweet flowers make the air fragrant.

And Thou! my divine Master, well-beloved Jesus! when Thou walkest among souls, come and rest in mine.

It is unknown to men, like a hidden spot in the forest, but it will attract Thee by the trees—that is, by the virtues that grow therein:

it longs to attract Thine Eyes and captivate Thy Heart by its charm; for it will offer Thee a thousand tiny flowers—very small, and hidden in the shade—which will draw Thee to it.

February 14, 1903

XCV

Jesus offers His Heart to us as a pattern of humility, because it is the homestead of Love, and love is the strongest incentive to true and deep humility.

February 28, 1903

XCVI

A labourer who is paid by the piece, works as fast as he can, because, the better and faster he works, so much the more he earns. The love of gain stimulates him every moment.

Thou! oh, my God! payest us "by the piece," since Thou dost not reckon by our days but by our acts of love and charity: yet—notwithstanding—what zeal do we show in our journey towards Heaven?

XCVII

The mason does not think himself a great architect when he builds a beautiful edifice by faithfully following his master's orders; neither is it becoming in a soul to take praise to itself for the building of spiritual holiness, raised according to divine teaching.

XCVIII

Why is it said that the soul of a monk knows nothing of the delicacies of love—the deep tenderness, the passion of loving? Why do people sometimes fancy they see in a monk, one who is cold and austere even in his love? Why should those who dwell in solitude be accused of cowardice in leaving the joys of social intercourse, as if their egotism were enough to fill their narrow hearts? Why should such things be said, oh! my God, by the very people who, knowing nothing of Thy Supreme Beauty, love only one person themselves, and are captivated by a single heart? They know simply nothing of the ardent love that may consume the heart of a monk!

Would they say, however, that a wild bird which would die unless it were free to enjoy the immensities of Nature and the boundless sky, has less life than the bird in a cage, which is satisfied with its prison? And wild flowers that grow in solitary places and are deliciously fragrant and brilliant of hue, are these less beautiful and delicate because in human hands they would die?

Now, the soul of the monk is that bird that demands the freedom of the empyreal heavens. It soars like the lark—it flies without fatigue—it delights in the far-off heights where all sight of earth is lost. It takes there its free pleasures and never leaves those privileged spheres unless obliged by its frail nature to descend. Ah! God Himself is the beautiful sky in which the soul delights to dwell, with Him, in prayer. If it leaves the earth, it is because it is cramped there—it flies because eaten up by Love—because no one else understands its insatiable need of loving; above all, because nothing can fill or satisfy its heart. Therefore it flies in search of its God because love constrains it.

Again, the soul of the monk is that fragile flower that wilts and withers at its contact with the world. Take away from a loving heart the object of its love, and you will see it close up, pine away, and soon succumb under the trial. The true monk's heart is passionately in love, not with any creature, but with God. If then, his All be taken from him, and a trifle—a mere nothing—be given him instead, how can he go on living? And, if he should die from this, will it be said, then, that it is because he knows not how to love?

March 1903

XCIX

An interior soul is a world of holy thoughts and ardent aspirations, of deep virtues and exquisite tendernesses. It is a mysterious solitude which the Master inhabits and which He cherishes. He alone knows its charms. He revels there in the thousand tiny tokens that He finds there for Him.

Yes; the soul is indeed a hidden world. In fact, very little emerges to the outside, beyond a few words or sighs! Perhaps these exterior appearances may show certain points of character and moral bearings; but that deep mystery of the soul itself, so wide spreading and so rich, remains unknown. And this is the cause of every interior soul being subject to misunderstandings, false judgements and harsh criticism on the part of others, who do but catch a glimpse of, and wholly fail to understand that hidden world.

C

I feel that a soul in union with Christ, grows and develops slowly, but surely and regularly, like a wild flower of the fields, that expands in a fertile soil under the continual gentle action of the sun and dew. But yet! oh! dear Jesus, how slow the progress of the soul seems when its impetuous ardour would fain hasten its course towards Thee!

CI

The soul prays in different ways according to its needs; but it has only one song—the song of love, which is that of divine Praise; and this song becomes so sweet to it that it finds all its happiness there and all the food for its life. Joyful, joyful song—which drives all real sadness away from the soul!

CII

When a man is growing old, his body suffers at feeling its fresh and youthful life is gradually becoming feeble. But the soul should never grow old. Yet how few there are who escape from the depressing influence of the flesh as it weakens, little by little under the weight of years! How many are these who keep that youthfulness of soul that is, perhaps, even more charming when the forehead is wrinkled and the hair white?

Where this is seen, the secret of that perpetual youth is to be found in the love of God; in the care the soul has taken to persevere in that love, to preserve in it all the eager refinement, all the doting ardour, all the passionate tenderness of a heart still in its teens. If the soul knows how to foresee and ceaselessly to forestall the least wish of its Divine Lover, and to show Him its devotion by numberless little attentions, that soul will remain always young, because it has never lost the freshness of first love.

August 3, 1903

CIII

When one cannot fall in with the wishes of our companions and do as they say, because they are unreasonable or against the directions of superiors; then we must act according to their best interests, doing what we judge to be most useful for them. This, also, is Obedience.

CIV

Little flowers that are never seen, give out much fragrance whilst they escape notice. Certain souls are like that. All who come near them fall under the charming spell of their sweetness and virtues; most of all, that mildness which is the very perfume of holy souls, and the "good odour" of Jesus-Christ.

September 28, 1903

CV

It seems to me that recollection is the possessing of oneself in God, Who dwells in the centre of the soul. When that possession is perfect, the soul can do no act without perceiving at once whether it is acting *in* God and *for* God: and from thence comes the importance of recollection for the soul that wishes always and only to do what is most pleasing to God.

October 7, 1903

CVI

A soul may be disturbed and troubled. I know, O God, that dark days are kept by Thee for the soul that loves Thee sincerely; days when the darkness of evil hides the brightness of Thy Countenance, and the soul is troubled by the darkness that surrounds it; when temptations disturb the whole being, in such wise that there seems hardly any will left with which to overcome and quell the revolt of one's whole self, bringing it within the limits of Thy law.

Oh! Lord—how storm-tossed such a soul is! "I feel," says the poor soul, "I feel as if a furious ocean rages within me! My love of Thee—oh! my God, is battered like a frail boat in a tempest. The sky is black, no star shines to guide me to shore. My passions, like immense waves run high and carry me on their crests, only to throw me again into the frightful abyss, and a hundred times they suck me under, to fling me up once more. The depths seem to open to swallow me up, the great waves threaten to undo me, to dash me against the reefs!"

Oh! how storm-tossed that soul is! and from whence can salvation come, unless Thou, oh! Lord, art sleeping in its midst, as once in Peter's boat, and unless, by a word, Thou wilt make "a great calm," when the tempest is at its highest?

November 11, 1903

1904

CVII

The further a soul advances on the way of perfection, the more it finds its food in God, free from all that is not Himself. This food is the Bread of the strong. The weak, too, draw their food from God, but from God reduced, if one may say so, to the level of their weakness…and, in the same way, the priest, the shepherd of souls, must be able to adapt himself to the individual needs and capacity of his flock, and not lead all in the same pastures.

February 28, 1904

CVIII

In the moral world as in the physical, men of small stature try to make themselves look taller than they really are. But the truly great try, on the contrary, to diminish and efface themselves. Others, again, rest satisfied with their own mediocrity. This, in the life of the soul, is a very sad disposition.

February 29, 1904

CIX

What hast Thou done to my heart, oh! God, that my soul is no longer able to contain the burning love it feels, and which it finds itself unable to express?

I catch a glimpse of Thy supreme Beauty and of Thy gentle kindness, whenever I have a chance to contemplate the harmony of Thy works and taste their sweetness in solitude with peaceful Nature. And, yet, what do I know of Thee, Almighty God? What is man, that Thou speakest to him thus? to him, who trembles at Thy very shadow?—is he anything more than the field flowers that praise Thee spontaneously, without any thought of their own beauty? Yes—my whole being tells me that man is greater in Thine Eyes than the merely natural creation; but I know, likewise, that he owes this to Thy merciful kindness, which has been more liberal in gifts to man, than to the flowers! Be Thou forever and ever blessed for this!

CX

As the fullness and freshness of the fountain's water will not quench the thirst of one who is not able to drink of it; so the sacred character of an action is not enough to sanctify him who performs it in bad dispositions.

March 1, 1904

CXI

A sympathetic nature necessarily attracts others, and becomes a centre—more or less admired. But, let your soul, which is really only desirous of attaining God and His love, not fancy itself to be holy in the degree in which it is admired. In fact, it is very often natural qualities that obtain praise, more than personal merit.

O great God! if it happen that I should please others, do Thou look at the depths of my soul and see my firm resolution to please Thee alone. On this point I look for the help of Thy Grace, that I may never fail.

April 10, 1904

CXII

Why should so much zeal, initiative and intelligence be lavished on material things, whilst constant opposition is shown in questions of moral improvement? What inconsistency there is in human pride!

May 6, 1904

CXIII

I know the blissful happiness of a soul that owns no other master than Divine Love!

But one who is much afraid of suffering would not envy its lot, for the thirst of love is a ceaseless suffering. If God shows that loving soul but a glimpse of Himself, the fire that consumes it becomes white heat—if He plunges it into the obscure darkness of Faith, hiding Himself from its gaze; either the soul pants after the Object of its love, and only Support of its weakness—or else it is overcome by self-reproach, and bitterly weeps over its infidelities which have separated it from its God.

Those who know not these raptures, and who seek for God in punctilious but cold performance of duty, not asking for love, would perhaps advise others to go more simply, and to have done with feminine ardours and dovelike sighs. "What good is in all this?" say they! What good?—ah! at least it is a proof that the soul knows God is its Father, and the tenderest of fathers—that the soul wants to love and serve Him as a child, and not as a slave, and that consequently, the Holy Spirit of adoption breathes in it!

And it is a proof that the soul knows Jesus Christ, and sees in Him, not a Judge who comes to lay down a law of iron, and condemn us at His tribunal, but a Shepherd, full of tender care for His sheep; a gentle Master, ready to comfort us in our toils, and teach us the joy that is to be found in His service; a compassionate Brother, a celestial Spouse desirous of responding to the warmest and most confidential aspirations of a soul entirely devoted to Him. Again, it is a proof that the soul has given itself unreservedly to God. Since it ought to love God with its whole heart, it will not give Him a dry heart, unable to beat in unison with His; but a burning heart, brimming over with youthful vitality, freshness and enthusiasm!…And that does not prevent it from loving with force, fidelity and constancy.

But it is the loving heart alone that understands this language, for it is the expression of what is really passing within it, and in such a case it is necessary to have felt, in order to understand.

CXIV

If a poor man should make his way into the palace of a king, he would be surprised at the sight of the riches accumulated there, and even so full of admiration that he might not give a thought to the king himself, through enjoying the wonderful sights. However, if he were ushered into the royal presence to find the king simply dressed, in a room with ordinary, perhaps austere furnishings; and if that prince should receive him distantly, the poor man would no doubt wish to go back and look again at the lovely things he had left.

Now, this is just what often happens to a soul that seeks God. When it takes its first steps in the ways of prayer the king makes its paths pleasant; it feels attracted by the ineffable consolations, and tends with all its might towards that land, as yet unknown, but so full of promise of bliss.

The danger is, that this soul may pause on its way, to taste these delights, and imagine it already possesses God, when it has only just crossed the threshold of the door to the divine palace of prayer. It must now go on, and arm itself strongly, for surprises are awaiting it. It will find its God; but in such solitude, so deep and so retired a solitude that Faith alone can lead it to Him. Nature will be wearied and cast down: the soul by Faith will see its God there, it is true; but that God, so veiled to the eyes that seek Him and long for Him, is often in appearance without anything that attracts—even cold, repellent and frowning!

There is a danger for the soul when in this solitude, and this danger is lest it should go back to those consolations it has left behind. It must now act in exactly the contrary way, and, by its holy perseverance vanquish the Lord. If the time of waiting causes aridity; if the soul can no longer in tender affection pour out before God the heart consecrated to Him alone, if God seems not to notice the loving longings of His creature, the soul must nevertheless not weary in well-doing; it must increase and multiply its aspirations, it must augment its fervour, and go on doing this unweariedly, until it overcomes the aloofness and shatters the barriers of its Lord.

May 8, 1904

CXV

The most painful thing that happens to a well-intentioned soul that is careful to please God before anything else, is to feel the severe or mean judgements of those who are always looking at the shady side of other people's actions in order to criticise them pitilessly, and, very often without either right or reason.

May 19, 1904

CXVI

As the bee flies from flower to flower, seeking honey in each fragrant chalice, so my heart is irresistibly drawn to dive into hearts to draw from them the riches of divine love. But, if souls resemble flowers, it happens sometimes that mine finds no booty: for the bee does not only find well-opened blossoms: there are some that remain closed, hanging down their heads, and many more withered or shrivelled. Souls that have never known the beauty of love are like these.

May 22, 1904

CXVII

I think that those who truly love God, do not find it difficult to be on good terms with their neighbours. But I except those who pursue us with too human an affection. For a soul really in love with God could not approve of affection of that sort, and, generally, would find it insupportable. Perhaps this is the reason why, though it is easy to be sweet and pleasant to all others, yet with such friends as these the soul becomes cold and hard.

CXVIII

Why is the soul a dwelling that must be lived in? And, above all, for the monk who truly seeks happiness? Because every man worthy of the name, needs a home where he can enjoy the companionship of one or more intimate friends. Well—the monk having, for the love of Christ relinquished the right to make a natural home and there satisfy the affections of his heart—where shall he retire to taste the joys of friendship which his ardent nature craves, except into the solitude of his own soul, which has become exclusively the temple of God? But how small is the number of those who know the sweetness of that divine love that is enjoyed in that secret sanctuary?

June 7, 1904

CXIX

What is meant by intimate friendship? True friendship is the affectionate union between certain souls, based on the mutual understanding they have of each other.

A man who feels the need of being loved and seeks intimate friendship, ought to make himself known with sincerity, just as he really is.

Intimate relations soon spring up between souls who are made for mutual understanding.

Although, among men, intimacy generally springs up between a very few—most often between two only—yet it can unite a larger number of souls. Jesus Christ is the intimate Friend of all souls who love Him, and in the degree of their union with Him, do they share in that privilege.

June 10, 1904

Aspirations and Thoughts

CXX

Because a flower has grown, hidden and unknown in solitude, it does not deserve less admiration and love from him who finds it. It is the same with a soul that God has hidden from the eyes of men by giving it a reserved and retiring nature to the extent of hardly ever finding means to express the depths of its feelings. That soul either does not speak at all of the things that really occupy it and the yearnings that inflame it, or does so very rarely; and yet it is often these very yearnings and those things, that make it experience the need for some intimate relations with souls who can understand it.

If you meet with such a soul and guess its state—go forward and meet it halfway. Will it not be,—even to yourself, a very great pleasure to open your heart and to love it?—all the more because, of itself, it would not know how to venture out of its isolation, nor how to gain the happiness of feeling itself loved and understood? Do you love that soul! love it with all the unselfishness of your heart. Do not ask for words, because that is not the way to gain confidential friendship; but ask it to have the same supreme desire and need as yourself: viz: that of seeking God and loving Him alone.

June 19, 1904

CXXI

How painfully, at times, suffering distends the heart! how grievously it oppresses it! No other relief is left it but that of pouring out its troubles.

But is it right for a generous heart that could bear its own burden in silence, to resort to the solace of speech?[78] Ought it not, rather, to suffer and be silent?

---

[78] Of course, there is here no reference to the confidence given to the spiritual director of that soul.

A Benedictine Soul

This was a question that I could not decide for a long while. Now, I think I have found an answer that suits the difficulty completely.

First, there are souls who ought to be silent about their interior pains: among these are holy souls, in whom the extraordinary action of God works things that they feel are difficult to reveal. Then, again, there are cowardly souls who seek to lessen their troubles and lay down their crosses by talking about them. Lastly there are those who, from want of proper feeling and reticence are always ready to evaporate and dissipate their minds by talking, to anyone and at all times, of what they have to endure.

But there are some who *ought* to speak of their interior sufferings, and among these we reckon weak souls whose pains are increased by keeping them to themselves, and proud people, who make it a point from vanity, never to do so, as if they were above the weakness and miseries incidents to human frailty.

Now we come to those I have particularly in view. These, although not yet walking in higher paths of perfection, still seek nothing else but God alone; in all things and at all times wishing to please Him, and consequently believing it a duty to reserve to Him the knowledge of what they suffer, so that He alone may know of and be gladdened by the heroic patience with which they wish to carry the Cross, following Jesus Christ.

I certainly believe that a soul that is strong and generous, ought to embrace its cross with great love, and, whatever may be the weight that God sees fit to lay upon it, not to put away the least item by its own will. I believe, too, that such a soul may not seek anxiously to find a sympathiser who would understand it, nor be disturbed or agitated if such a friend is not to be found. But, if the soul feels sincere and constant love of the Cross, and bears it with feelings of peaceful joy, as soon as God sends it a competent friend, let it open out all its griefs, and be free from all fear of displeasing its divine Master. The effect of this outpouring will not be a lightening of the cross unless God wills it to be so, Himself; but the soul will gather new strength to bear its trials, and will go on its way towards Him with greater joy and more abundant peace in the midst of suffering.

1905

CXXII

My soul often feels a longing to speak and sing. But its words seem vain and its song inharmonious, and nothing can overcome its timidity but the knowledge that it speaks and sings for those it loves.

The Land of My Love

Is there any young soul that is not moved by the beauty of nature?

Those solitary forests; those bold rocks that in their proud sterility seem to raise their heads to heaven, and hang suspended over the valleys—that torrent that roars on its desert way—all these cannot fail to make our hearts beat with joy and admiration.

But how is it, oh! God, that countries seemingly so enriched by Thee with special predilection, do not often hold our hearts and thoughts captive, whilst others chain us by bonds so delicious and so innumerable that they make of that land truly "the land of my love"?

I ask Thee this question, oh! good God—and yet Thou hast no need to tell me again, for in Thy kindness, long ago Thou didst teach it me! The Land of my love is so because, beyond the charms of nature, there it is that I have found the delights of friendship; of family love: there it is that I had my place at the family table and above all, enjoyed the sweetness and intimacy of home life. There, a friendly hand led me through the wide woods, full of the tranquillity and peace of God—along those beautiful white roads, so calm that one felt unwilling to speak in going along. That loved hand led me through desert valleys, on to the plain where the horizon spread afar—led me by mountain footpaths;—a beloved voice taught me the legendary names of the ancient rocks. Often, when the sun went down over that lovely landscape and our friendly intercourse, it left us to the happiness of finding ourselves again in the sweet calm of home.

Aspirations and Thoughts

This is what makes "the land of my love." And when, after long absence and having almost given up all hope of seeing it again, I return to that Land, it seems as if I had never left it. I tread again the path to the church, that we used to tread so joyfully among the early mists, in answer to the call of the village bell. How well we know the footpaths on the mountains, though scarcely visible! The trees by the wayside tell stories of our past. Here and there, we meet the honest face of an old friend, some countryman who greets us! We recognise the turns in the valley, and each bend of the river recalls some event of our past…everything around us seems to live.

And then—oh! dear Land!—if we must leave thee again!…perhaps for long; what can we take of thee with us? Nothing but a fleeting and futile memory?

No: love does not live by such ephemeral things only! No: my love for thee will survive the ravages of time, for it is founded on that divine part of man's nature which never passes away. Events and happenings go by, but amongst these the soul remains firm and steadfast like some old oak in a forest whose hoary trunk has never known a blow from the axe, although, perhaps a hundred times the foresters have cleared the brushwood and lopped off the branches here and there. And, in the same way as these forest kings continue growing, and only let the rotten branches fall off, so the soul grows, ever rooting itself in the Immutable, only giving over to forgetfulness the faulty feelings of sinful nature.

How then, oh! beloved Land, is it possible that my heart, or any heart that has once really known thee, can ever suffer the memory to fade or be effaced?

How many a time have I not paused, my soul silenced in admiration, to hear thee speak of thy Master, with sweet and irresistible persuasiveness? It was the transparent river that seemed to praise the Lord for the purity of its waters, sometimes gaily singing its happiness, it rushed from bank to bank, sometimes glided pleasantly among the silken grasses...it was the wonderful clothing of the mountain, where, among the rosy heather and golden broom to the gigantic and austere larches, all grew in one harmonious pell-mell of colour and size. It was the great silence of evening, when Nature, robed in mist seemed to take its rest under the starry sky, and in the profound calm the vibrant voice of the Infinite can be better heard.

But—oh! Land of my love! know that if thy beauteous and powerful voice was better heard and more loved than those of other equally favoured places, if thine accents more than those elsewhere have announced new emotions and fresh ardours within the soul, it was because, *here*, one was not alone to tremble at thy touch, but because other souls, warmer than one's own, were there also! Thou, oh! Land, hast seen the blossom of holy friendship expand in thy pastures—a flower that was incorruptible and delicate as the works of God—breathing the sweetness of love, the perfume of divine Charity. And now, why should I say any more?— the heart has sung like the bird sings on its bough. He who knows the voice will have listened and will say, "*It is he.*" A stranger may, perhaps, hear—but will weary of a song which, for him, will have neither charm nor harmony.

Maredsous. September 7, 1905

CXXIII

The fruit of self-surrender is found in the ineffable peace and sweet repose which the soul, by the effect of loving confidence in God, keeps in the midst of difficult, and sometimes inextricable situations.

November 18, 1905

Aspirations and Thoughts

1906

CXXIV

I have recognised his voice! 'Tis he!—He sings again, fitfully—for those who know how to hear!

Where can a better image of profound peace of soul be found than in the evening of a fine day? Contemplate nature on an autumn evening, at the moment when she still smiles in her summer tints, but with a something calmer and sweeter than in her impetuous youth. Contemplate this nature in repose, when the sun sets and disappears below the horizon, inflaming all the pure, deep sky with its great fiery disk. The earth is dry; grass and flowers, wearied by the heat of the long day, seem to call for the coolness of night. The air is calm: no breeze stirs, to bear along on it disturbing echoes of the doings of men. If any human voice or sound of bell is heard, it is an invitation to prayer, or some peaceful song rising from a little cottage with the smoke of the hearth-fire, and both together spread sweetly, mingling with the silence of the evening. Nothing can rob this peaceful hour of its irresistible charm and delicious rest; and, whilst all is wrapped in tranquillity the light mists can be seen coming back to earth, which the heat of the morning sun had drawn up. They fill the valley and spread over the meadows, and, when their veil has been delicately laid over the grass and the little bowed heads of the sleeping flowers, then Night is upon us; dark Night, when all keeps silence, save only the Voice of God.

Perhaps some bird fitfully raises a plaintive cry, or a brief melodious warble; but the softness of its accents, soon silenced, does but deepen the feeling of the immense peace which surrounds and penetrates the soul.

I paused on my way one evening, struck by the grandeur of this sight; in the silence of my soul I contemplated it, and I heard Thy Voice, oh! my God, speaking to me in the depths of my being and impressing on me forcibly the great truth that peace transforms all things and inundates them with divine sweetness!

April 8, 1906

CXXV

As the river flows into the valley; as the flower eagerly raises its head to the light; as the timid hart seeks the deepest solitudes—so, oh! Lord, does my soul overflow in Thee, that it may be ever filled with Thy splendours, that it may lose itself forever in those divine solitudes created by Thy Presence within itself: "Ecce elongavi fugiens et mansi in solitudine."

Maltebrugge, July 20, 1906

Aspirations and Thoughts

1907

CXXVI

Here below, the great mysteries of love are profound abysses of sufferings. Love only becomes a true mystery in the soul on that day when it reaches the inmost folds: and, love never touches these secret depths, without burning terribly.

Chateau de Bochryck, January 1, 1907

III

God's Note Book

Holy Trinity, Whom I wish to love with all my heart, with all my strength and with all my mind, I beg Thee to look upon this little Note-book and consider it as being an "Appendix of my heart"; into it I shall pour out all the overflowings of my soul and shall note down all my most intense desires.

May these lines be, before Thee, like a prayer forever for all who are dear to me.

This Note-book then, is Thine own

—"God's Note-book,"—and the first prayer in it is "MY GOD, I LOVE THEE."

God's Note Book

Maredsous, September 24, 1900

Oh! Lord Jesus, in gratitude for the lights Thou hast given me during this Retreat,[79] I promise Thee to do all things to sanctify my soul. I desire with most earnest longing to succeed in this, and I will it with a firm will. I feel an urgent need to show Thee my love in some way, and I do it now by renewing my vows with all my heart; those Vows which are the blessed bonds uniting me to Thee forever.

O most beloved Jesus, Thou alone knowest my soul, and canst clearly see how pride overflows it, notwithstanding all my failings that blacken it in Thy Sight. Thou also knowest what ravages are wrought there by my selfwill. If only I had worked hard at my own conversion since the blessed day of my Profession! But henceforth, from this very moment let us never be separated, oh! Jesus! From now, I will unite myself so closely with Thee that my mind may be Thine, and occupy itself constantly with Thee, unless Obedience or some reasonable call prevent me: and, even in that case I resolve that

---

[79] The exercises of this Retreat were given by Dom Columba Marmion and impressed its decisive attraction on the life of Dom Pius. *Vide Supra*.

my work shall speak my love for Thee in such a way that at all times my heart may be entirely submitted to Thine.

If Thou wilt give me the time I would like to hold a long conversation with Thee—but I cannot. Read, then, in my heart and be assured that I wish to unite myself to Thee; in Thy humiliations by a deep contrition, and in Thy Sacrifice by a perfect Obedience.

September 25, 1900

Holy Ghost, dear Guest of my soul, I have told Jesus that I want to love Him ever more and more. And now—Thou art Love—and I beg of Thee to go on with this good work Thou hast begun in my heart.

And, first, Thou knowest how unfaithful I have been to Thine inspirations, with the result that now, instead of being on fire with love, I am often like a lump of ice: and then, my faults have implanted pride in me to an extent that is really terrifying. I promise Thee now, that in future I will be very docile and give myself up to Thine influence and abandon myself to Thine action, only begging Thee to deign ever to guide me—as well in the Divine Office and spiritual reading as in all my other reading and studies.

Furthermore, by the merits of the Well-Beloved, to Whom Thou wouldst unite me, I entreat Thee to breathe into my soul a most intense longing to live with Him—so that seasons of dryness and darkness may not have power to chill my love for this divine Master, but may rather serve to increase it.

Finally, from today, oh! holy Spirit Whom I truly love, make me see that nothing is more beautiful than humility. I entreat Thee to hasten the moment when Thou wilt inundate my heart with this virtue, for I have understood Thine inspiration and it belongs to Thee to give that, which, of myself I could not obtain.

I am insistent—am I not?—and so will I ever be—because I love Thee, and long to be entirely, completely Thine own.

God's Note Book

September 28, 1900

Sweetest Jesus—at this moment I seem to have no more ardour in going to Thee—still, my Well-Beloved if my heart does not suffer from being unable to love Thee, yet I feel keenly desirous of burning for Thee with ardent aspiration. I am Thine, oh! Jesus, and Thy Spirit will unite me with Thee forever! That is why I throw myself into Thine Arms, as to the direction of Thy Spirit. Make of me whatever Thou willest, by Thine own immediate action, or by my superiors or by my brothers—do with me as Thou wilt, and I will try *to obey perfectly*. But, above all, I beg Thee to inflame my heart with the desire after perfection, and to teach me how to humble myself.

October 2, 1900

Oh! my God and my only Good! my heart is joyful, indeed, for Thou hast just made me understand that all is love; that nothing matters but *love*! Yes! I know this practically, and in future I will only live by love. I feel whatever we do by love, is done by the Infinite Love; and, in order to place myself entirely under the direction of the Holy Spirit in all things and everywhere, I wish for nothing but love.[80]

And besides, there is another grace for which I must thank Thee, my dearest Saviour: Thou hast given me a thirst for humiliations, in order to satisfy the desire I have to show my love for Thee. I am joyful because Thou wilt put Thine own spirit of humility into my heart which is so full of self. All that I *can*, I will do, oh! Love, in order that I may not put any obstacle to Thine action—in order

---

[80] This passage, if taken by itself, might perhaps suggest to a reader who is not previously warned, some controversy on the "way of love." In the correspondance of Dom Pius, explanatory passages will be found of his ascetic conceptions.

that I may love Thee truly—that is to say, humbly, and solely for Thine own Sake.

Yes. Oh! Lord—humble me—but do Thou sustain and bear me up—for the very least humiliation is enough to terrify me, so great is my pride. But, for love of Thee I accept joyfully whatever humiliations Thou shall send me, oh! my Beloved! For thus I shall be a little like Thee. I will love Thee much, and more sincerely.

October 11, 1900

Lord Jesus! Yesterday I seemed to hear Thee, telling me very softly, to occupy myself with Thee alone. I am not sure whether I understood Thee quite well: speak to me again like that, and I will do all I possibly can to concentrate on Thee Who art my only Love, all the powers of my mind positively.

Pursue me, until all that is not Thee, is quite destroyed in me. I wish to give myself up utterly into Thy Hands, and to have neither intelligence nor will, save to know Thee, to love Thee, to obey Thee and to humble myself. Make my heart love Thee, and, notwithstanding my resistances Thou wilt triumph over my very wretchedness—this is what I greatly long for!

Louvain, October 14, 1900

My good Master—everything around me is changed, and I feel that Thou only remainest the same: Thou; in Thy tabernacle and in my unworthy heart. I cling more closely to Thee; I will never leave Thee, nor love any else but Thee.

Holy Spirit help me, since for the future I am to study theology, and even natural science. I will apply myself to them under Thy direction, doing nothing without Thee. May I be impregnated by Thee, and may my union with Christ become closer every moment!

October 21, 1900

Thanks! thanks, my merciful Jesus! for now Thou dost allow me to communicate nearly every day.[81]

Oh! sweetest Master—can it be possible that Thou shouldest grant so ineffable a grace to such a poor, unworthy servant as I am? Grant at least, oh! God, I beg of Thee, that I may feel how I ought to humble myself for being, through my fault, so little worthy to receive Thee, and such unspeakable graces: once more I give myself up entirely to Thy Divine Spirit, Who will unite me to Thee.

On my own authority I should not dare to approach Thee so often. I do so by obedience, trusting myself completely to Thine Arms, and leaving to Thee alone the care of filling my heart with contrition and humility in proportion to the immensity of Thy benefits. Unless Thou shouldst do this, how, indeed, could these benefits bring forth the fruits of glory and sanctification for which Thou wilt certainly look?

October 22, 1900

My Jesus, I desire to give myself to Thy Church by love—even as Thou hast given us an Example.

By my holy vows I am completely Thine: so it follows that I should take to heart the interests of Holy Church, that is to say, the interests of Thy most loving Heart, in such a way that my life, which is wholly liturgical, may be one prayer for Thy beloved Spouse.

And, if I pray for particular intentions, I will only do so with a view to Thy glory and at the suggestion of Thy Spirit Who guides me in Thy holy love. My heart belongs to Thee, oh! Jesus, and must only love as Thou lovest, and enlarge itself to embrace all Thine intentions, and contain all that Thou wouldst place therein. May Thy holy

---

[81] At this time the Pontifical Decree on daily communion had not yet been promulgated.

Spirit, then, dilate my heart, which is powerless by itself, and shed abroad in me that charity of which He alone is the Source, so that I may be able to fulfil the duty which henceforth Thou layest upon me of loving souls after Thine own example in so far as a miserable creature such as I am, can do.

January 27, 1901

Thou, oh! Jesus, art my only Good: why then does not my whole being strain after Thee alone? How is it that my soul, which desires only Thee, is not yet filled with Thy love? Oh! Beloved of my heart, either I am mad, or Thou alone must possess me!

Show me my infirmities so that Thou mayst replace them by the strength that is Thine own. Come! Jesus, Come! I love Thee, I want Thee. Am I not yet sufficiently abandoned to Thine Arms? I do not know how to give myself more fully to Thee! I hope for all from Thee, my good Master. But if my hope is still too weak, increase and strengthen it Thyself, so that in future I may have no life but Thine.

March 25, 1901

Behold, oh! Lord, I give Thee my whole self. From this day forward, do Thou grow in my heart even as Thou didst grow in the Bosom of Thy Mother![82]

April 18, 1901

Most holy and eternal Father, Thy divine Son has taught us that no one can come to Him unless Thou dost draw him, and that none shall be lost of those whom Thou hast given Him. I beg of Thee, therefore, in the name of the mutual love Thou bearest to Him and Him to

---

[82] Alluding to the Consecration that Dom Pius made on that date. The Feast of the Annunciation. *Vide supra.*

Thee, to offer me and all whom I love to This Divine Son, begotten of Thee, so that being born again in Him, Thy Word, we may have a share in the eternal glory which He gives to Thee, and that we may thus be sanctified in Thee.[83]

Eternal Son, whose holiness is equal to that of the Father, Thou hast promised that "when lifted up from the earth, Thou wouldst draw all to Thee." Draw me, then, to Thee, oh! Well-Beloved of my soul, that, being fed by Thee I may live by Thee, even as Thou livest by Thy Father.

Holy Spirit, Who didst descend upon the Virgin to accomplish the mystery of the Incarnation of the Word, come down upon me, oh! Thou joy of my heart and strength of my soul! Impregnate me, to the end that Christ may grow in me! Thus, by Thee, the closest union may be effected between my Saviour and my poor soul, inflamed by Thy love.

Oh! adorable Trinity, look down and behold how I burn with longing to glorify Thee—see how my soul shrinks into nothingness—see how little it is—how it abandons itself utterly to Thee!—and yet it loves Thee only a little. But, to prove my love, or at least my desire to love Thee, I now protest that I love Thee by the Heart of Jesus and by every one of the souls on earth...and therefore I will bring them all to Thee. To this end, Christ Jesus, Only Object of my desires, I take refuge in the Bosom of Thy Father, and, in His Name I give Thee all these precious souls, that not one of them may perish. Then, uniting myself to Thee, I offer them all to the Father, for the eternal honour and glory of the most adorable Trinity.

Oh! my God, I feel the need of laying open my soul to Thee, although Thou seest it better than I do. If I only considered my own

---

[83] This deep thought—a quite legitimate one—is, that union by an act of love is effected to the eternal generation of all things and of oneself, in the Word.

mental powers, which are so narrow and so limited, I should be silent before the consideration of Thy Majesty and my littleness. But my heart feels that Thou art here present at my side, and deignest to listen to me. Besides, my heart cries out louder than my mind,—calling to Thee and telling Thee that Thou, oh! my Lord and my God, art my sole Good, my Joy, my Happiness, my Life, my All, and that outside of Thee I can find naught. Yes, I assure Thee, this is true, as Thou Thyself hast told me—love must do all within me. It must kill my pride, and, with my pride, all my vices. It must give me new life, purify me, and make me labour and suffer for the good of souls. I burn to love—and I wish for nothing but that which Thou willest for me.

June 22, 1901

Oh! my beloved, my sweet Mother Mary, Thou knowest how greatly I wish to love the holy Trinity…but, for this I need Thy help—come to my aid, or I cannot succeed.

I am Thy child and have the happiness to have always belonged to thee—my heart belongs to Thee far more than to myself. I long for Thee to give it to Jesus continually, just as thou gavest Him Thine; and for this I want to make a sweet compact with Thee, oh! Well-Beloved Mother. All my happiness lies in giving myself up to Jesus, but my weakness in such that I cannot make the complete surrender I wish for; and so, now, once for all I place myself in Thy heart, where Thou wilt deign to give me a tiny corner, wilt Thou not? And, as Thy self-surrender is perfect, *thus*, mine will be the same as Thine. I love to do this, to show Thee my gratitude and tenderness, for it was Thou who didst first teach me to walk in the way of intimate union with Thy divine Son; and it is to this Jesus, hidden within Thy Bosom, that I consecrated myself unreservedly, this year. Thou wilt understand that I cannot draw near to our only Beloved, without feeling myself on Thy tender heart. And, finally, Thou—Thou alone—knowest the recollection and carefulness I ought to have, in order that Jesus may grow in my heart, as Thou didst bear Him in thine.

With Thee, then, would I live, for I have but one want: and that is, that I may belong to Jesus in order to belong to our Father. So I make my compact with Thee, to walk towards Jesus by Thee only: and on Thy part I beg Thee to make of me a good and holy priest who will live for nothing but his sacred ministry.

One more request I would make, oh! my dear, good Mother and that is, to teach me the sufferings endured for us by Jesus and by Thyself. I have wanted this for a long time, and have asked Thee to do so. Thou knowest that every evening, when I kiss Thy scapular, I kiss Thee. But I must say no more, for, when I begin to speak with Thee, I know not how to end.

I love Thee a thousand-fold, dear Mother.

June 24, 1901

Well-beloved Mother, I feel that Jesus unites our hearts, and I am always thinking of thee. I can and will never again take a step towards Jesus, our One Beloved, unless Thou leadest me. He will not want to see me without His dear Mother and mine! Yes. I love Thee, sweetest Mother and I long to imitate Thy virtues; or, rather, I will imitate *one* specially, which is the recollection with which Thou didst carry Jesus within Thee. I, also, have received the divine Word; so I ought to be very watchful and diligent in doing the work begun in my soul; for, if I should be negligent, our well-beloved Himself would suffer. For the moment I am well-disposed, I wish and will only that which our Good Master wills and wishes. But I need Thy help so that at all times and under all circumstances these sentiments may so possess my soul that nothing can ever separate me from my divine Spouse.

As I said before, I long to know the sufferings endured by Thy heart and by That of Jesus. Tell me, tell me the pains I have caused to Him and to Thee; show me the frightfulness of my faults, so that I may become less unworthy to be Thy son and more earnest in loving nothing but our dear Saviour. I will work with all my power to make others love Thee, oh! sweet and good Mother, for I believe I do love Thee dearly.

July 26, 1901

Dearest beloved Jesus, Thou hast shown me two faults I must correct in myself. The first is an excessive effusion, and the second, a foolish way of laying down the law about everything.

I shall have to make serious efforts to cure these two failings, for they are deep down in my natural character. I put this work into Thy Hands, and present myself to Thee, hidden in the Heart of Thy Immaculate Mother so that Thou mayst help me to accomplish it. That tender Mother is willing to receive me and offer me to Thee, to the end that Thou mayst take care of a soul which, notwithstanding its littleness, longs to love Thee.

Grant—oh! Jesus and Mary so tenderly loved, that my soul may ever gush out near to you both in your Hearts, which shall ever be the only Friends of my heart. Do Thou show me, whenever Thou wouldst have me open out to any other, and when I ought to be silent. And next, teach me a right reserve in speaking. I do really know nothing at all, and it is incomprehensible, how from bits and odds and ends of ideas, my self-sufficient mind builds up theories, as if to demonstrate and enlighten others much better informed than myself. I ask Thee, then, to teach me the reserve and modesty that belongs to true humility; for my one desire—yes, my only desire is, that nothing displeasing to Thee shall be found in me: but I wish to belong to you Both, in every item, however small, so that I may constantly glorify the Most Holy Trinity, Whom I adore humbly in my nothingness and Whom I love in the Hearts of you Both, which can never be separated, the one from the other. I love Thee, Jesus—I love Thee greatly—I love Thee a thousand-fold—I love Thee so much that I wish I could cry it out over the whole world.

I love, Thee, Mary my Good Mother, I love Thee dearly. I love Thee because, through Thee I can love Jesus, and I wish that all the world would love the good and tender Mother of my dear Master.

July 28, 1901

Thy Heart, oh! Jesus, is a stronghold that must be entered. Once within, Thou wilt protect us. Thou art the watch-man Who never leaves his post, and we can safely give ourselves up to the thousand follies of our love for Thee.

But, oh! blessed Jesus, tell me how I can make my way into this holy Enclosure. I have gone up with Mary; why are the gates still shut against me? Do not, oh! Best-beloved, do not look at my wretchedness, which, in spite of Thyself is enough to prevent Thee from receiving me, but take me in, to the Furnace of Thy divine love, and Thou wilt see how all that has displeased Thee in me will be quickly consumed. Thou knowest, Only Beloved One, that I desire but one thing only—the Glory of Thy Father. All that I ask of Thee must only serve for Thy Glory, oh! my God. Grant that all my being may labour to increase that glory. By this I mean, help me to love Thee as much as Thou wouldst have me to do.

October 1, 1901

Holy Virgin, a long time ago I made Thee Queen of our little cell, and so shalt Thou ever be, for in this little sanctuary I wish to unite myself with my divine Spouse under Thine eyes, my Mother. The cell of my heart has belonged to Thee for long. Grant, oh! tender Mother, that I may faithfully stay in this holy solitude, where I can love Thee and our Jesus so freely and so tenderly.

A Benedictine Soul

October 3, 1901

Oh! my only Good, my dear Jesus, I so deeply feel that in me there is nothing that is good! My life has been so careless ever since my youth—and I *could* have done so many acts of virtue! Thou hast done everything to keep me from the worst falls—this I know and believe. I wish everyone could see how it is Thy Grace alone that has prevented me from perdition long since!

Oh! Love of my soul, I want nothing any more but Thee! I renounce all creatures—all possible pleasures and enjoyments. Draw me to Thee, my Well-beloved, even to the heights of the Cross.

I ask myself if it is not too bold in a wretched creature such as I am, even to wish to have no other thought but only of Thee, Lord Jesus—and to have the ambition to become a great saint? I grieve to think that even with the help of Thy Grace, I may only sanctify myself by halves (through my own tepidity). But is it vanity on my part to wish to become a great saint, or perhaps through an illusion of the devil? All these are the thoughts that would, indeed, disquiet my soul if, by revealing them in this way, I should not confide myself entirely to Thee.

November 5, 1901

I see, my Well-Beloved Jesus, that Thou wouldst have no other friend for my soul than Thyself. And, on my part, henceforth I desire none other. Thou art my Treasure; be Thou my All. Is there still anything in me that does not completely belong to Thee?—anything I would not give up to Thee? I do not think so, good Jesus! Thou hast taken all; even those that were most dear to me! I have naught; Thou alone remainest to me. But Thou art fully sufficient, Beloved! Give me Thy divine Heart that It may be my Confidant, my Friend, my Guide, my Master. All I want is to lay my head on Thy Breast and hide my soul in Thine, oh! Jesus, so that I may draw thence all the learning and light that I need, and the heat that is lacking to me!

And, finally, oh! my Beloved, do Thou think of me as a very little child who can do nothing whatever of itself. If Thou dost not carry it, how can it go? If Thou dost not purify it in Thy Blood, how can it please Thee? This is why I want one thing only, to love Thee. I want nothing but Thee, oh! my Love—I want Thee, quite alone, my Well-Beloved, so that together with Thee, I may be the son of our heavenly Father and of our good Mother, Mary!

November 8, 1901

Most dear Jesus! I truly wish for but one thing only, and that is, that I may do whatever is pleasing to Thee, no matter what it may cost me. I wish to love Thee and never to take away from Thee the least little part of my being. If it should be Thy good pleasure for me to give myself and lay open my heart to anyone,—to whomsoever Thou willest—I will do so, just as far as Thou wilt have me to do.

If, on the other hand, Thou wouldst have my heart known only to Thee, Thou art my Well-Beloved and my Treasure, I will show it to none but Thee, my divine and only Love. I ask only that Thou wilt take me into Thine Arms, to accomplish all Thy designs forever—and that Thou wilt give me Thy Divine Heart.

I can say no more, oh! my Jesus. I love but Thee alone, I love Thee dearly and will ever love Thee as much as so poor a creature possibly can.

November 9, 1901

I know it is already too much for such a poor creature as I am, full of myself and natural pride, to be able to give itself up to Thee, oh! good Jesus. After this, it ought to be silent and await Thy good pleasure. But, oh! my Well-Beloved, Thou dost Thyself so compel me to love Thee, that my soul is *doting* on Thy Heart!

It cannot hold itself back and wait humbly; it urgently feels the need of obtaining from Thee the fulfilment of the one, only desire that remains to it, that of possessing Thy divine Heart. This is not for my own satisfaction, but rather to the end that my whole being may belong entirely to Thee, and that Thou mayest dispose of it as Thou wilt. As so few men are completely Thine, I wish to be so for them, and to love Thee with Thine own Heart, to make up for them.

December 13, 1901

Dearest Mother, sweetest Virgin Mary, my poor, tiny soul has an immense need of loving: for to live without a friend who is in union with it, is impossible. I have no such friend and yet my heart is used by many, to serve as their friend.

Give me a friend, then, but none other than Jesus. I do so long to love Him, yet I love Him so little! Open the way, and take me into His Heart, teach me the immense love that fills with which it burns the grief and anguish It endures for us. I think, oh! gentlest of Mothers that it is not possible to abandon myself more to Him than I have done, for, as far as I know, I can find nothing in me that is not His already, nor wishes to be His alone and submissive to His Will. However, to make sure, in future most sweet Mother it is in union with Thee that I give myself up to Him. Thou alone shalt give Thyself up to Him in my name, in my behalf, saying again those same words that Thou didst say to God by the Angel-messenger, "Ecce ancilla Domini, fiat mihi secundum verbum tuum."

Every time I give myself to Thee, oh! beloved Mother, saying the words; "Tuus sum ego, o Benigna," and thus abandon to Thee all my being without any reserve whatever, Thou wilt give me over to Jesus, with the same dispositions as Thou didst give Thyself. For I renounce and reject everything that is not given over to our sole Treasure, our only Love, our dearest Jesus! He, and Thou, dear good Mother, possess my heart. Pierce it with the arrows of Love, so that it may die whenever Thou willest. *Grant that I may die of love!*

I must say a little word to Thee, oh! good Jesus, for vehement desire oppresses my heart. Oh! Thou knowest how impossible it is for me to live without Thee, my best-beloved! Thou art, indeed, installed within my poor heart, and there I ever find Thee—but without knowing Thee well enough! A true friend opens his heart to his friend—be Thou my Friend, my Confidant—the only Friend of my soul which is so little and so unworthy. Open to me Thy Heart and teach me how to use the riches to be found there. For, Lord Jesus, I wish every action, every movement of my whole being to acquire an infinite value by its union with the movements of Thy Sacred Humanity; and this, for the glory of our Father and Thine, and for the good of Holy Church.

Live, then, in my heart, and inundate all my being entirely with Thyself—for my love is Thine—only Thine—*utterly without reserve.*

December 14, 1901

My Well-Beloved Master, I have often met with friends who would, I think, have answered to my need of someone with whom I could be on intimate terms,—those of real friendship such as would make me love Thee more, my beloved Jesus—but Thou Thyself hast invariably put some hindrance in the way, both before and since my entrance into the monastery. Still, the desire grows in me!

Could it be, oh! Jesus, that Thou wouldst design to fill my want Thyself and be that Friend of my poor little soul? Oh! if indeed it might be so—let me know in some way! Make known to me the secrets of Thy Soul, the burning flames of Thy Heart, for, in that mutual acquaintanceship is the basis of true friendship. Thou knowest only too well, how completely I abandon myself to Thee, ever to doubt of my content, my joy, whatever Thou mayst make of me. Steep my soul in Thine, for I can no longer live alone and there are others for me to help.

My thoughts never leave Thee; may my heart never feel anything else but Thee, always and everywhere; thus we shall become true friends, my only Love, since Thou condescendest to draw nigh to a wretched little creature like myself!

I love Thee greatly in desire—but, it seems to me, so little in reality. Oh! uncreated Love, let this be changed!

December 17, 1901

Until now, my best-beloved, my soul drew near to Thee as to a sweet solitude, a place of rest. Now, it longs to see and possess Thee evermore, but only with the design of offering Thee a heart wherein Thou mayst repose, whilst I shall work, fulfilling Thine orders.

I am a poor little creature, but Thou art so good, Lord Jesus, that I think I may be able to console Thee for so much coldness and ingratitude that meets Thee from the world. This I will do by lying still in Thine Arms and caressing Thee as a little infant fondles its mother, and thus makes her forget her troubles. When, then, shall I receive Thee into my heart and thus keep company with Thee? I long to make my heart ready like a dwelling for Thee—well-warmed—and where nothing can offend the holiness of Thine Eyes!

Whether I recite the divine Office, or whether I suffer anything, my intention shall be to solace Thee in the person of my brethren, in the souls of all members of the Church, militant or suffering, and to bless Thee in the Saints who surround Thee. If Thou givest me consolation, I intend to accept it and apply it to Thyself in my poor person, and, by returning to Thee every joy Thy love gives me, I could thus show a more ardent and more tender love. Thou knowest that I have offered them all to Thee, long ago, oh! most loving Saviour. It is Thyself I seek, oh! my God, and not the pleasure of serving Thee. I want but Thyself alone, and nothing else besides Thee.

Teach me to be gentle and humble, so that all I come near may feel joy and consolation in seeing that they are loved with true divine charity. For it is always Thyself that I long to console and cheer in them, oh! infinite Love of my soul, my only and supreme Treasure!

When, oh! my God, when wilt Thou come and satisfy me?

December 21, 1901

Oh! Jesus—ardently beloved! who can tell the depths of the feeling Thou hast inspired in my poor, unworthy soul? Its desires are unmixed, oh! divine Master. It is Thyself, and Thyself alone whom it yearns after! Bad as I know myself to be, I can truly say that I could not long after Thee more earnestly than I do—oh! divine Love of my heart!

My soul is so greatly in need of Thee that I do entreat Thee to open Thy Divine Heart to it. *That* is the Object of all my desires—give this adorable, this burning Heart to me!—see how I am less than nothing without Thee; still, in my nothingness and abjection I love Thee madly—and love Thee thus, as many times as there are souls in heaven, on earth and in purgatory; for, each of these souls being a tabernacle of Thine, has all my love! Grant that I may love Thee, oh! tender Jesus.

December 25, 1901

It was on this day, oh! Jesus, that Thou didst dawn upon us, to show us that God is Truth, that God is Love; Thou didst come to bring the divine Fire with which the whole world should be inflamed.

Oh! Word Incarnate, Beginning of all light—of all heat—Oh! burning and consuming Furnace, I give myself over to the flame of divine Love. May that flame be mistress of all my being, and help me to overcome all movements of my lower nature, which are still so active in this poor heart which I abandon to Thee.

I cannot possibly, oh! my Jesus, my only Treasure, throw myself more completely into that Furnace of Love which consumes Thee from all eternity, and yet—I am still just as cold as if I knew not the fire of Thy love! Do not delay, oh! divine Master; I wait for Thee, for I know that Thou wilt come: but my soul longs after Thee like one overcome with parching thirst.

December 26, 1901

Oh! Jesus, Thou knowest, and I also see, that, without Thee I am but a dried up flower, without perfume or beauty or any attractiveness whatsoever. Thou lovest me, and I tenderly love Thee, in Thyself and in every separate soul, oh! Jesus, my only Good. I trust myself to Thee utterly, and long that Thou wouldst rest in my poor heart as in some little solitude, where Thou shouldst hear no complaint, where Thou shouldst never be offended, where Thou couldst forget all things— even to console me! Come to my poor little soul; it longs so eagerly to offer Thee a resting place; narrow, it is true—but warmed with the warmth of Thy divine Spirit; where Thou mayest rest Thy holy Head; where I may always love and caress Thee, and whence I may draw from Thine opened side loving words wherewith to console and heal the wounds from which Thou dost suffer in souls. I do, indeed, love Thee, oh! my Jesus and my All. Do with my heart whatsoever Thou wilt—unite it to whomsoever Thou wilt, provided that it may never be separated from Thee in the least degree. For I have none other wish but to possess Thy Heart, after Which I yearn!

January 1, 1902

Oh! immaculate Mary, I belong to Thee this year in a very special way, since Jesus has given Thee to me as my Patroness. I love Thee so much, dear Mother, that I never want to leave Thee. Guide me in the path of holy self-surrender, in that of holy love, so that nothing may remain in me that does not belong to Jesus and to Him alone.

January 2, 1902

I feel, oh! beloved Master, that the one motive for uniting myself to Thine adorable Heart is that I may dare, in Thy Company to approach to the Holy Trinity.

I adore Thee, oh! Blessed Trinity and give myself up entirely to Thee as Thou dost condescend to ask for my poor heart. Eternal Father, make me one with Jesus. Give me to Him so that I may, indeed, belong to Thee.

1st Friday, January 3, 1902

My dearest Jesus, today I enter, in thought and desire, into Thine adorable Heart, to make there a Retreat, preparatory to the solemn vows which I am to pronounce on March 21.

I will live in Thy Heart, so that I may sink deeper and deeper into It with the earnest desire that this blessed work may begin at the end of this Retreat. I wish to keep my soul in humility, sweetness and charity, as Thou willest. Do Thy work in me, my only and beloved Treasure.

January 7, 1902

My good Master, Thou usest me as a poor little tool by which to help others of my brethren. I beg of Thee, in Thine own Name, never to let me be the least hindrance to any of Thy loving designs—either by unsuitable word or by behaviour. I will oblige myself to keep very close to Thee at all times and in all circumstances, to listen to Thy orders, execute Thy wishes, and never to do anything but what is pleasing to Thee. Having said this, beloved Lord, I will never go back upon it, but walk on always with Thee, and following exactly the direction of my Father and of my conscience. Fill my little soul each day with ineffable tenderness towards all men, but above all towards those who, by Thy Will, are nearest to me. I love Thee so much, oh! Jesus, sweet Saviour—I love Thee dearly, but give me the warmth of love that is necessary to enable me to kindle the fire of Thy love in those where Thou wouldst have it burn.

January 9, 1902

My God! my God! when shall I love Thee? When shall I truly know the Heart of Jesus? Oh! Father, look upon the least of Thy sons—he is burning to please Thee! Mercifully draw me to Jesus, my Only Good! speak to me of Him, because whosoever has heard and has learnt of Thee, goes to Him. I can do nothing but love—and, alas! I love so little! I am devoured by the need of loving, and my soul is so limited. I have despised all things, renounced all things to possess one only Object, the Heart of my Jesus, my adorable Master, and That seems so firmly closed against me that I cannot get in—nor so much as look into It.

Have mercy on me, oh! my God! do with me as Thou wilt. I wish to love nothing but what pleases Thee.

January 11, 1902

O! Jesus, my only Love: why is my soul not all for Thee, without any motion but for Thee and in Thee? I have the greatest desire and need of knowing Thy divine Heart! Now I have come so near to making my solemn vows and to go up to the Altar—and yet—oh! adorable Jesus—where am I? It seems to me that to be away from Thy Heart is to have no part, no rest anywhere. Oh! Jesus, look and see at last, whether my heart is not yet completely in love with Thee: see how I must absolutely love Thee!

My Jesus, my Jesus! I want to love Thee. Yes. I will love Thee alone, in all things and in all places.

January 14, 1902

My good Jesus! Thou dost condescend to take my poor little soul as Thy Spouse. Thou knowest how unworthy it is of such a grace, and that of itself—of its own part it would never dare to presume to such an honour! But it is Thy Will, my sweet Master, and that is why I, Thy little Spouse, am dying of longing for the day of Espousals. Do not delay that union, oh! Jesus, for what can I do without Thee?

Many thoughts come to me every day and I write down what I can.[84] My intention in this is to pass on to other souls what may be of use to them—not with the view of pleasing them—for it is Thou only Whom I wish to please.

January 24, 1902

My divine and tender Master, my soul feels like a little fountain fed by Thee. Those whom Thou leadest to it drink and quench their thirst because they find there the living water of Thy love. Oh! Jesus, I will let them come and drink their fill peacefully, the little brides of Thy Heart: even if they ought to become inebriated with love at the fountain of my heart which would remain cold, itself: I will never put any obstacle in their way, nor become envious of them. No, rather will I efface myself in future, as soon as a soul shall be entirely given up to Thee, so that Thou mayst possess it; and thus Thy poor little tool will give Thee a proof that he has understood his mission.

He, himself, depends on no one but Thee; he is in Thy Hands, do with him as Thou pleasest. He has but one wish, that he may live in

---

[84] This refers to the "Thoughts and Aspirations," and not to these "Notes," which were never shown to anyone.

Thy Heart, so that he may become warm therein himself, and then to Thy little brides he can impart warmth also.

January 27, 1902

Oh! Well-Beloved of my soul, I will give myself to all, with all the tenderness that I feel: one thing only would I keep, and that consists in depending on none other but solely upon Thee, oh! my Love!

February 8, 1902

Ever since my birth, oh! God, Thou hast surrounded me with hearts that can love greatly and delicately, and that love Thee much. Grant to me, now, the power to cherish for Thee all those souls who sincerely yearn for Thee. Oh! my good Jesus, Well-Beloved Master, see how much time these good brothers of mine take up! How am I to know Thy will, in such difficult circumstances?

After all, my only Beloved, Thou knowest that in all these long conversations I neither seek nor find any other comfort than that of helping Thee in these dear souls. If, in any way I am in the wrong about this, look at the dispositions of my little heart, which only wishes to please Thee—Thee alone—my most merciful Saviour. Until now, Thy Heart has been the only Refuge for mine, which is sometimes in great need of rest. I wish to meet Thee always with a smile, my dearest Master; and make no account of the weight that presses on my heart, for it is Thou Who permits it. Nevertheless, oh! Jesus, so tenderly beloved, let me pour out my heart into Thine, so that it may be able to continue helping other souls, by its difficult mission of acting always as a fount of refreshment and as sweet oil to soften and to soothe them. But, I repeat it once more, best-beloved of Masters, I am so devoted to Thee that I want but one thing only, notwithstanding my numberless faults. This my one desire is, that I may please Thee—Thee alone—*quite alone*: and, if

I should please anyone else, that it may only be in the way and in the degree that Thou willest. I love Thee, I will love Thee more and more, oh! most lovable, merciful Saviour, but do Thou give me the strength to bear the waves and billows of suffering which threaten to overwhelm my poor heart. Give me deep humility, which I need that I may find it right when anyone judges me unfavourably or treats me slightingly—for I am but a little insect that deserves to be scorned and got rid of. Give me so much gentle meekness that I may be able to hold my ground in the combats to which my heart is given up! In short, I wish to be entirely in Thy Hands, oh! my divine Jesus, and that Thou mayst make of my soul whatever shall be pleasing to Thee. I want to follow Thee by love, and never again to leave Thee. Hold Thou my soul, whilst shedding upon it sweetness, meekness and humility.

May 22, 1902

My dearest Master, the cross I have now to bear is known to Thee: it costs me very much and pierces my heart—how deeply is known to none but Thyself.

Ah! well. Today, so near to my ordination to the subdiaconate, I offer this cross to Thee, and wish to bear a thousand more, if Thou shouldst think well to lay them upon me. I know not what else to give Thee, for nothing is left me but Thyself—Thou, the sole and whole Love of my heart! I renew the act made at the moment of my solemn Profession, and offer also my whole will to make the Vow, of which I have thought, if it should please Thee.

Finally, my God and my All, I beg Thee to imprint on my heart the virtues necessary for the ministry to which Thou Thyself callest me. Of myself I do nothing good, and my only wish is to give my little soul up to Thee entirely, so that it may submit as perfectly as possible to Thine action.

And, oh! my sweet and tender Mary, do Thou take into Thy Motherly Arms this little weak infant, who cannot walk; who does so much that is faulty and who yet—notwithstanding all this, is called by his vocation to so high a ministry. To Thee, then, oh! beloved Mother and to Thee, dearest Jesus, I make my urgent petition—which is—*that I may never go up to the Altar without remembering how sublime is that act which I am about to fulfil there.*

This, oh! Jesus, is my whole desire. Thou, alone, knowest how much I love Thee.

June 22, 1902

The cross is sometimes heavy, oh! Jesus. And I thank Thee! The soul suffers, but I am given over to Love, and Love will make of that soul whatever pleases Him.

August 11, 1902

Divine Master, it is now only a few days before I shall be ordained deacon. I know something of the greatness of that Order and of the responsibility belonging to it. Ah! well, my only Love, look on my poor and sinful soul, and see its wretchedness in order to cure it. In the meantime I want to tell Thee, my Beloved, that my poor little soul, alone before Thee, has never drawn back from placing all its joy in Thee. Now, more than ever, Thou, indeed, sufficest for me, my divine Jesus. I want no one beside Thee, but I do wish to win souls to offer to Thee.

My own, my only Love, come into my poor heart and open Thine to me! I feel all my unworthiness, and that is the claim to Thy merciful goodness. Grant that I may love Thee! Grant that I may love Thee, oh! Jesus, in this dwells all the strength of my soul—and—what great need it has of strength, since it accepts the Priesthood for Thee! That means, that it accepts a share in Thy Passion. Yes, I love Thee. A thousand times I love Thee, and I cannot do otherwise. Grant me to feel as Thy Adorable Heart feels, so that I may be what Thou willest.

Take possession of my poor little soul, for it belongs to Thee, solely and unreservedly,

August 15, 1902

Mary, most tenderly loved, once more I come to give myself to Thee, and the measure of the gift is just that of my whole being.

Take me, oh! sweet Virgin, and form my soul to the sentiments of a true priest.

Above all, I beg of Thee to help me to fulfil perfectly all that appertains to the office, and to acquire Obedience, according to the spirit of our holy Father Saint Benedict. Preserve my body in perfect purity.

I feel all the importance of the terrifying step I am about to take, and how great are the obligations attached to it. Thou only, with Jesus, canst help me to fulfil these duties. I depend only upon Thee, sweet Mother, and on Thy merciful Son. I am so hopelessly weak, and my heart is so full of yearning!

October 5, 1902

Well-Beloved and sweetest Master, today I came out of Retreat and I wish to thank Thee for all Thy merciful and gracious kindness in my regard. My firm and sincere will is to enter yet more deeply into the solitude of my soul, or, rather, into that of Thy Sacred Heart. There I wish to fructify the seeds which Thou hast so plentifully sown in me during these days.

I believe I shall cooperate in Thy divine action, and act according to Thy good pleasure, my only Beloved, by offering to Thee, as principal fruit of this Retreat, a firm will to perform the Divine Office with the perfection required for so sublime a function, and I entreat thee, Oh! Jesus, to give me understanding to do so. I wish to immolate myself so completely by gratitude, to the praise of the most Holy Trinity, and of Thy Sacred Humanity, that I may appear before the Eternal Father and before Thee, as a pure victim of praise, trained according to Thy life-giving spirit. These are my desires as to the Office. But, in order that I may be always in such a state as I wish to be during the Office, I humbly beg of Thee, Sovereign Lord of my soul, to keep me at all times in perfect conformity of my will with Thine. And here I renounce in particular my own opinions and judgements. If, now, Thou givest me the strength, my Sole Good; I will lead a life of love—all love. May my poor heart be Thine, and Thine be mine, my Well-Beloved Master. I beg of Thee not to delay the moment when love shall unite our souls, and when I shall at last be able to be pleasing in Thine Eyes, and offer Thee unceasing thanks. Look upon the desires of my heart; never do I wish to joy in anything but the doing of Thy Will. Thine adorable Will.

May equal thanks and gratitude be Thine, dearest Mother. Hold me in Thine Arms; keep me under Thy Maternal protection. I depend upon Thee to lead and guide me, so that I may find Jesus. Show me Him Whom I have so long sought after. I love Thee, good Mother, I love Thee with my whole heart.

October 11, 1902

My Well-Beloved Master, behold me. I am now in the year of preparation for the Priesthood. Thy holy Spirit alone can make my soul ready to receive so great a grace. I humbly beg of Thee to take my whole self into Thine hands. Behold me at Thy Feet with all the powers of my mind, and will, all my health, and every one of my actions, even the very least, whether good or bad, in order that Thou mayst purify and rectify them. I ask of Thee, my Love, to make my will so conformed to Thine that they may never be separated in anything whatsoever. This is the only, real, supreme desire of my heart.

Oh! most dearly-loved Mother Mary, this year is consecrated to Thee. I count upon Thee with full confidence that Thou wilt make of me a holy Priest, after the Heart of Thy Son, and in union with Thine.

February 7, 1903

It really seems to me that no one loves me and that I love no one, in the way that makes friends, for, although I turn on every side, I find no consolation but in Jesus, my sweet Spouse. I had given Thee my soul as a little garden where Thou shouldst be the only Visitor, where the flowers should breathe their perfume for Thee alone. And, behold! Thou hast brought in other souls, who have seen many things in my garden, whilst I, myself, have taken no pleasure in this their visit! Still, oh! best and dearest Beloved. Thou art ever the only owner of my garden. Bring anyone to walk in it that Thou dost wish. All whom Thou sendest shall have full liberty even if they gather the flowers and deprive me of them. I will never seek for consolation in anything else but in Jesus. I feel it is impossible for me, for Thou hast taken possession of my soul so entirely that there is nothing left for me to dispose of. If, at any time, my soul should escape again, take back Thine unfaithful Spouse, who neither loves nor wishes for aught but Thee. Thou art my Love, my All—my Good—but also my Cross—amiable, sweet and welcome—my cross, because Thou woundest my heart and then leavest it to sigh.

March 17, 1903

Good Jesus—rise on my soul like the early sunrise on a beautiful, fine day. I pine for Thy light, divine Sun of truth. Flood my longing soul with Thy heavenly brilliance and Thy devouring charity. I long for Thy charity and I need it, just as little buds need the sunshine after the long winter.

May Thy warmth, the fire of Thy love, the flames of Thy burning Heart warm, inflame, devour all my being—making virtues germinate and causing me to grow in Thee, its divine Master, its adorable Model, its Life, its Joy, its Love, its only Beloved, its All. Come, oh! come! ineffable Love; forget my sins, and look not on my merits but on the riches of Thine, and the boundless extent of Thy Mercy.

March 25, 1903

What is my poor little soul before Thy Face, oh! Thou my God, so good, so holy, so just, so kind! What is it, Almighty God? However, it is the work of Thy Hands. As Thou didst create great trees, so Thou didst also make little flowers; all come from Thee, all belong to Thee. My heart, little as it is, comes from Thy Hands, and Thou hast made it capable of loving Thee. Though it is soiled, it longs to love Thee, oh! my God—and so much the more as it has failed in fidelity to Thy love. See, then, the longing that hurries me towards Thee,—the desire to please Thee—oh! Thou—single Love of my soul! What can I do to impel Thee to inflame me with Thy boundless charity?

I entreat Thee, with all the strength and earnestness given me on the one hand by my utter depths of need, and on the other by the abundant love of my unrivalled Spouse, I entreat Thee, oh! Lord, to inflame my soul with the fires of Thy love. Then it will expand and grow as spring flowers do, as soon as the sun appears. May Thy grace make my soul fragrant with the good odour of Christ, so that Thou alone mayst enjoy it, and be pleased by the true likeness of my soul to Thee. I am envious of the beauties of Nature which expand so quickly, whilst my soul often lingers and languishes in the chill atmosphere of sin. However, oh! Jesus, Who art the Treasure of my soul, the precious Pearl in Whom I find my beauty, the Sun Who warms my heart. Well-Beloved Spouse, I am

Thy little bride—a servant who would not push her attentions to indiscretions, but only to console the Heart that beats with flaming heat for me, and whose warmth I yearn to share. Listen, then, to the voice of Thine own love and not to mine, which is but the faint echo of Thine, oh! passionate Lover of my soul. Together with my beloved Mother who this day conceived Thee of the Holy Ghost, I wish ever to be united to Thee, oh! Word Incarnate, and this, through the renewed operation of the Holy Spirit, and under the protection of the Most High. Hide me in the Light of Thy Countenance, oh! my God, so that my soul may at last enter into that deep Retreat, Thy very Self—into that solitude where the flower grows without danger of being trodden underfoot, into that peace that nothing in the world can disturb, and where Thou canst work out my sanctification without let or hindrance. May my soul gather its powers together in recollection thus by Thy grace, oh! Jesus, so that from this day forward, by the help of Thy sweet Mother, it may only live by thinking of Thee, submitting to the influence of Thy divine Charity, never missing or wasting any grace whatsoever, and transforming itself into Thee, to become a true and holy priest, according to Thine adorable Heart, which I ever wish to please; as my beloved and only Spouse.

April 1, 1903

Nothing can satisfy my soul but Thyself, oh! good God. I feel no pleasure but in Thee. Thou alone art my Consolation, in Thee alone I joy, who art my soul's supreme Good.

Have pity on my weakness, and on the helplessness of my poor heart. Let Thy mercy overcome my sins and vices, destroying them utterly so that no trace may remain. Implant that firm faith into my soul which is the principle of true love, and draws it to practice all virtue.

A Benedictine Soul

April 18, 1903

Sweetest and most beloved Mother! I have perfect trust and confidence in Thee. Thou knowest the extent to which I belong to Thee. Thou holdest my poor soul in Thy blessed Hands; place that soul now in Thy gentle Heart, and in that of Thy dear Son. Give me such deep humility as may make it natural to me to feel no right thought, no good interior movement comes from myself, but that it is Thy Divine Son, the only Love of my heart, and Thou, best of Mothers who inspire all this within me, and give me the strength to accomplish it.

Oh! why?—yes—why should I live with my mind fixed upon earth, whilst that earth is but the passing dwelling of my body, and that the only and dear resting place of my soul is my Jesus, and in Him alone.

Now, on the eve of receiving Priest's orders, blessed Virgin, draw my mind—draw me, I entreat Thee, from earthly preoccupations, hide me in the Presence of God, so that His divine Look may penetrate very deeply into my heart, may wound me with the wound of holy love, and may at last unveil to me the mysteries of charity hidden in the suffering Heart of Jesus, and in Thine own! Thou knowest the importance, the necessity of all that goes to make a good priest: above all, Thou knowest how immeasurable is the humility which the priesthood demands. And so, I come to Thee—oh! fair and most fair—most pure and immaculate—most blessed and beloved Virgin Mary! I come to Thee with the confidence of a poor little child—to tell Thee that now, more than ever, Thou art my most dearly loved Mother: but that I am a child whose poverty must move Thee to pity—and whom Jesus wills to make a priest!

Thou knowest all the rest, dear Mother; I love Thee from the bottom of my soul. Tell my Beloved that I love Him, for I do not know how to tell Him any more. From this day forward let me live in Retreat under Thy Motherly direction; instruct me, and change whatever ought to be changed.

April 27, 1903

Oh! Jesus, I hunger—I am famished. Feed Thou my soul, that it seek no other pasture than Thyself.

May 9, 1903

My gentle Mother, most holy Virgin, my soul seeks its God. How long must I wait for that blessed moment when Thou wilt give Thy son to me? Notwithstanding the sighs of my poor heart, and the longings that make me suffer so much, I remain patiently in Thy keeping, on Thy holy Breast, and in Thine Arms. My whole confidence is in Thee, and I know Thou wilt give me what I have asked, because I am Thy child and will love nothing but God. I love Thee dearly, gentle Mother!

May 11, 1903

My God! my God! How greatly I love Thee! I know not how to tell Thee, and yet my soul wants to repeat it to Thee over again a thousand times.

May 14, 1903

Lord Jesus! I feel that my life is a mass of imperfections and sinful inclinations that offend Thy holiness, and of infidelities that retard my union with Thee. Still, merciful Saviour, Thou hast given me the firm will to do only what is pleasing to Thee; I am more and more determined and will try never to fail in this. Forgive my utter frailty and blot out from my poor soul all that may displease Thee there. I seek only Thee, and love but Thee, and will take pleasure in Thee alone, my Love and my All.

May 21, Ascension Day

Oh! beloved Saviour, I want to pour out my poor soul today, in Thine: and first I would tell Thee, oh! holy Love of my heart, that from today I shall withdraw into the Cenacle and there abide with Thy Mother (and my Mother, too) with the Apostles, and particularly St. John, my very dear Patron. I wish to persevere in continual and fervent prayer, in order to receive the Holy Sanctifier abundantly. This Retreat will be continued until my Ordination. It will give Thee an opportunity to perfect in my soul the work Thou wouldst do there, before that day. I will seek, then, to live in deep and burning humility, to leave Thee full liberty in my poor soul; knowing that, with my good and gentle Mother, Thou wilt keep and care for it lovingly. But, to the end that Thy merciful goodness may be poured out unreservedly into it, I implore the prayers of all the Saints, specially those of St. Joseph, of our holy Father St. Benedict, of my sweet patron St. John and of my glorious patron in religion, St. Pius. They know what they must do to help me. Every day, from now until the Ordination I will say the Litanies of the Saints, to beg their protection. I want my whole life to be a perpetual Act of Thanksgiving for all Thy loving-kindnesses, and benefits, oh! my Jesus!

September 10, 1903

My Blessed Saviour, since I have been a priest I feel more keenly than ever, the extreme wretchedness of my sinful soul. Have pity on me, oh! my good Jesus! No matter what comes, I will never take any pleasure but in Thee, my divine Love. When can my sinful soul blossom in Thee and become really fruitful? Do not, oh! gentle Saviour, do not forget this little outcast! I have such great need for the sweet warmth of love. It seems as if Thou wouldst plant my soul in the strong soil of suffering, and feed it with pain. Very well. Do with it as shall seem good to Thee; but sustain my weakness. I will, indeed, suffer with

Thee, so that I may love with Thee and like Thee—for Thou art the Life of my soul, my Well-Beloved—its Only Beloved and its All.

November 8, 1903

Oh! Jesus, my soul is cast down by its want of Thee, and, far from possessing and being satisfied by Thee, it feels overcome by dryness and temptation. Keep my poor heart for Thyself alone, Lord Jesus: guide my soul's flight towards Thyself alone, so that it may never return to the vanities from which Thou hast saved it. Listen to the cry of my weakness. Why hast Thou, from the very beginning of my religious life, put into my heart the one desire of living closely united with Thee, and yet delayest to take possession of that which has given itself entirely to Thee?

December 12, 1903

My God, I feel alone. I do not possess Thee as my soul so greatly needs; and I find no creature that can enter into and share the inexpressible feelings which overwhelm me. Lord Jesus, my sweetest Love, do not abandon a poor creature who loves Thee, seeks for Thee, wants only Thee; and who possesses nothing else, because Thy love is my one and only need.

March 1904

If I should describe how my love progresses towards Thee, my God, I should compare it to the faulty growth of a badly cultivated plant. A young plant may sometimes be met with, that comes up very slowly and weakly, as if everything around it hinders its growth. The leaves as they unfold are soiled and imperfect, the blossoms open halfway, but have neither scent nor hue. What can be wanting since every sort of care is lavished upon it? Ah! what it wants is a lifegiving breeze; the blessed influence that wakes up dormant nature, rousing it from stupor and reanimating its languishing vitality. Give it *that*, and you will give vigour and life to the poor plant.

The divine, lifegiving Breath is just what is wanting to my soul. Thou hast given me so much, oh! Lord, but Thy generosity has only served to fan the flame of its desire to live by Thy Holy Spirit. Oh! Jesus! I entreat Thee, do not delay any longer, for my soul sighs after Thee "quasi cervus ad fontes aquarum." Without Thee, it is like a dried-up land where no water is. Come and quench my thirst. I need no other fount than that of Thy Love, and await from Thee alone the fertilisation of my soul. Hear the cry of my heart: Thou alone art its Master; to none other have I ever given it than to Thyself! Why then, dost Thou not take possession of it? Once more I give it up to Thee, even more than ever. I abandon every other care into Thine Hands, but the one sweet yet crucifying care of loving Thee alone.

March 7, 1904

When, good Jesus, when will the day come—that blessed day that I have called and yearned after a thousand times, the day of Thy manifestation to my soul, the day when Thou wilt enter into possession of that which belongs to Thee? I cannot believe that it is far off, for the ardent love and longing in my heart tells me that it is approaching. Yet, the waiting time is long, my sweet Spouse, my beloved and merciful Jesus! I know that from the moment Thou shalt enter into it, my soul will be mercilessly tortured by Thy love; I am aware of the deep intensity of that divine suffering, and still I yearn for it with all the energy of my being, and I call out for it so loudly that, oh! Lord, Thou must answer—unworthy though I be, that Thou shouldst hear me!

Oh! kind and gentle Virgin Mary—my beloved Mother, give me Thy Son!

March 8, 1904

When the sun reappears after the winter, the flowers bloom everywhere and the grass is green and fresh...all this with a spontaneous ease that is astonishing. When I look at this sight, I sigh after the day when the Sun of Justice will arise on my soul; for, if I turn towards God, a great multitude of faults and failings offend its inward eye, and I see very clearly that true life and spiritual health can only be the work of Him whose divine light and holy warmth bring frozen souls back to life. And when will that longed for moment come for me—oh! Jesus?

March 10, 1904

My only and Well-Beloved Master, to show Thee how strong is the heat of the love that drives me towards Thee, I promise Thee to blot out from my mind and my heart all that might distract me from Thee. Thou, and Thou alone must be my occupation. To this end, and to trample more under foot the sins that prevent me from looking up to Heaven, I will in future keep my eyes on the ground as much as possible, so that the eyes of my poor soul may never turn away from my Beloved.

And, finally, oh! Jesus, to show Thee the sincerity of my love, I will make a point of loving particularly those, who, naturally, are disagreeable to me and cause me annoyance...

My God! when shall I love Thee?

March 11, 1904

Today, oh! God, I feel how great is Thy Goodness in having given me an Angel Guardian—and so, my good Angel, touched by the care thou hast taken of me for so many years, I come to beg thy forgiveness because I have so often forgotten Thee, and to thank Thee for all that Thou hast done for my poor soul, and for all that Thou wilt do in the future. As a proof of my gratitude that may be worthy of Thee, I have thought of something, the value of which Thou well knowest. I make Thee a sharer with me in the celebration of the holy Mysteries, so that, together with myself Thou canst glorify God supremely. And, since I cannot expressly name thee during my Mass, I intend, every time I say "and all the saints," to give to thee the first place among them. This is the gift I make to thee, oh! holy friend of my soul. I beg thee to constitute thyself as special Guardian of my senses, so that my eyes (above all) being closed to the things of the world, I may entirely belong to our Beloved, the Master of my heart and of my mind. Do thou keep all my soul for Him, unreservedly.

Oh! Jesus, do Thou keep me wholly for Thyself! I wish to console Thee by the intensity of my love. I do want so much to love Thee—grant that I may do so. I am Thy very own—as a victim with whom Thou canst do whatever may please Thee.

March 13, 1904

The more determinedly I close my eyes to the thousand nothings that surround me, the more I feel that Jesus-Christ, the divine Light supersedes the light in darkness of mere creatures, which no longer can illuminate the depths of my interior. And this hidden life and complete forgetfulness of all useless things, does not in the least embitter me, but rather softens and sweetens my soul, which needs it so much. My opinion is, that nothing else can satisfy my soul but contact with Christ, its true Love. In that sweet intimacy my soul joyfully expands, and this is why I sigh so ardently for the day when our intimacy shall be complete. Only Thou, Thyself, canst achieve this in me. In all sincerity of heart I can truly tell Thee Oh! Jesus, that I have no other desire. Thou shalt do all that Thou wilt with me, and, by the help of Thy Grace I will follow Thee everywhere. But grant, oh! divine Master, that I may know nothing else but Thyself alone.

God's Note Book

May 10, 1904

My God, Thou hast given me a heart of fire that tortures me ceaselessly, either by its excessive yearning after Thee, or by the privation of Thy Presence, there, where it seeks Thee. Is this a strange or illegitimate need?—this devouring want to be loved or to love? Indeed, I have sworn never to give my heart to anyone but to Thyself, and I know not how to attach myself to anything whatever, except to Thee—and—to be loved by Thee—Lord!

Oh! I believe that Thou lovest me! But I lack the experience of it, in myself; and I confidently pray Thee to fulfil it in my poor soul, for the love of creatures has never moved my heart. Often, I have been told that others loved me, or that I am generally liked; but, before Thee I am able to say, oh! my Spouse, that, if I have credited the speakers on account of their personal worth, I have never felt the affection on my own part, nor any consolation from their affection. Is it Thou—Thyself,—Who hast put this coldness within me, lest perhaps that love might have affected my heart and turned it away from its Supreme Good? I know not—but, at least, oh! Lord, fill the void of my soul by Thy love, so that it may ever be anchored in Thee alone.

June 24, 1904

Lord! Thou hast never let me be deeply touched by the love of any person. I bless Thee for it, because I hope that this action of Thine has attached all my love to Thee more closely. But—may I tell it Thee? I have great need of a Refuge! Give me that of Thy Sacred Heart, my good Master. I am a poor creature, do not be unmindful of my weakness. It is extreme.

July 18, 1904

All this month my soul has been often oppressed, burdened with griefs and strangely straitened—it comes now to Thee, to tell Thee all its interior and secret pains, and so to gain a little relief. But where can it find Thee, oh! Lord? How is it that, whilst every morning Thou comest down to my most inmost self—yet I cannot find Thee? Still, it is absolutely needful for me to have Thee intimately. I cannot do without Thine intimate Friendship, because, even when Thou givest me confidential relations with those I love, it seems to me that Thou dost not wish them to penetrate into my heart and make it enjoy a pure affection. How long must my soul endure this waiting, in which it is withered up—and its sighs have no effect but to tire it out?

My soul has sworn to belong to God alone—never to dispose of the least fibre of my heart, nor the smallest shred of love to anyone else but Thee—and now it renews its oath with fresh energy. God is very good; it seems to me a proof of His acceptance that I find nothing in which I can take comfort. And yet, from Him Who is my only Love, I cannot get any response to my advances!

Suffer me to make my complaints to Thee, my divine Master, for these issue gently and without bitterness from my heart. Yes—my heart is sadly oppressed—but—the more I suffer, so much the more I love Thee. May Thy Will be done, oh! good and sweet Master!

July 20, 1904

Almost always it seems to me that I love, without being able to persuade myself that I am loved. Thus, sometimes I feel much affection for some soul and make some confidences to it; and then I feel, if it were not for the sake of Jesus-Christ that I did so, I would not venture to make any further advance, so fearful am I of being troublesome to that other, of wearying or being burdensome to him. Is not this real suffering to a loving nature? It is constantly a suffering to me—I accept it fully, and will bear it until Christ Himself shall have brought some remedy to that state, in which affection is duly mortified. May my love ever be fixed in God.

God's Note Book

August 4, 1904

Whenever I re-open this notebook, it is a proof that my heart is filled with overwhelming feelings in regard to Thee, my Lord and my God; and, since it is always Thy love which inspires my soul with these vehement desires that make it sigh for very longing, all that I have written in "God's Note-book" is but the same thing, the one thing that I could go on saying over and over again, without ever tiring.

For more than a year past, Thine absence has made me feel a most painful void. I feel myself so alone, oh! my much longed for Jesus—and so weak without Thee; that, notwithstanding a keen want and an ardent desire of possessing Thee, my soul seems insensibly to relax without its efforts being successful in keeping it near to Thee.

And when I am at peace interiorly, it seems to me that this tranquillity is the fruit of a sort of carelessness or of blameworthy indifference.

My divine Master, have pity on me! If I suffer for love of Thee, I cannot doubt that Thou wilt take care of me; but—even so—human nature demands a response when it sings! I sing for Thee—I want a reply that shows me I am heard and understood. All my nature sings to Thee, oh! Lord—and Thou art silent so long that everything within me seems to fade and wither in Thine Eyes.

I do love Thee—and trust myself to Thee.

Maredsous, September 24, 1904

My good Master, I am coming out of Retreat, and on the point of beginning a new life that Thou hast arranged for me. I trust to Thee, beloved Saviour, to uphold my weakness in the midst of duties well adapted, as it seems to me, to distract my thoughts from continual converse with Thee. But, to make sure that I shall not be wanting in fidelity as much as lies in me, I promise Thee today to seek to live as much as I possibly can in Thy Company, with all the ardour of my soul, and all the energy of my will.

The means I will take, so far as depends on me, are these; every morning after my prayer or thanksgiving, I will arrange my time with Thee, foreseeing what may happen to distract me during the day, so as not to be separated from Thee, and to neglect no point of the holy Rule, which is the expression of Thy Will, and in keeping which, I prove my love for Thee. Help me, oh! divine Master—I am in Thine Hands without reserve. Give me that deep love for Thee, that charity which will be so necessary to enable me to teach those entrusted to me, how to know Thee.

May 12, 1906

I take up "God's Note-book" again, having left it for nearly all the two years I have been at the College.

I do a great deal of work. Perhaps more than normally I can do. I am told I do well, and I hear it from several quarters. But this appreciation does not touch my soul, for Thou showest me Thyself, that all I do is nothing and with what simple carelessness I do even this nothing and this is so impressed upon me, that at this moment I feel like shedding tears! I am terribly cast down, and reduced to nothing before God, and I believe that God is preparing some crushing blow for me, more than ever before; and this, not only in the depths of my own conscience, but also in the sight of others. As far as I foresee, it may be something hard and terrible. My pride shrinks, but my soul accepts fully, lovingly and without any reservation. Whatever comes, I will love Thee, my God. I need Thee and will seek Thee.

May 23, 1906

Oh! God, come to my help! I feel even more than ever, the extreme devotedness required for the office of Prefect. My heart is full of affection for the dear children. I give them everything. But I feel, nevertheless, that a prefect, however affectionate he may be, yet must have a certain coldness in the eyes of the boys. They may, perhaps, love him; but their love cannot gush out in that spontaneous flow of full confidence that opens the way for a superior to do much good.

Well! it's all the same! Thy love, and all the love of my being for Thee demand that I give my whole self to the work, and I do so, more than ever. Oh! Well-Beloved Lord, I will do it. May I entirely disappear and be forgotten, so that good may ensue, and Thy glory alone increase.

June 9, 1906

X…will soon be leaving us, and who will replace him? Thou alone knowest, oh! God! I have not his authority nor his influence over the souls of the children, and a man is needed who can sustain the good work. When I think of what is to be done, I get completely lost, and can only place my whole hope in Thee, Lord, for man fails at every point. Thou alone, oh! divine Master, remainest secure, and I do not doubt that these incessant changes and disappearances among us happen by Thy permission, in order that we may feel Thy immutability and providential power in all things.

June 13, 1906

This morning I spit blood again. It is the fourth or fifth time this has happened since I have been in the College. Before then, I had never suffered in that way, and these accidents do not trouble me. However, I mentioned it, to make my mind easy. I shall take as much care as I can, so that I may not become a burden to the Community. But Thou knowest, my God, it does not please me to use these little considerations in my own regard. I fear my own inclination to ease, which will know how to take every advantage. My poor soul may be lowered even more by weakened nature, and this is why I beg Thee, Lord Jesus to note that I condescend to these necessities only for love of Thee. More than ever I long for Thee alone: no other fire shall warm me than that of Thy love. I will be only that Thou wouldst have me to be. Notwithstanding all my numberless faults and unpardonable negligences in Thy service, I always keep, by Thy grace a determined and forceful will to please Thee, and Thee alone. But I feel all the burden of my incapacity. This is why I entreat Thee to take possession of my whole being, and thus to answer to the sole longing of my heart.

June 17, 1906

Lord Jesus! I so often feel the need of a real, deep, tender affection in my soul. But I have sworn to love none but Thee. So I beg Thee to see, in these needs of my heart, which I reject and renounce for love of Thee, another proof of my fidelity. I am young, ardent, passionate. Is it surprising that my heart leaps at the sight of what is lovable? However, if it is moved; it shall never, by my own will, beat for any other heart than Thine own. Every time that I feel my heart moved by any creature, I wish that it may rather bleed and suffer than enjoy and succeed anywhere but in Thee.

Support my will, Lord, for I dread my own weakness. Warm my poor soul, inflame my cold heart, for I dread coldness and need heat. Give me, oh! Jesus, the vital heat of Thy love, or grant me grace never to fall from Thee if Thou keepest me at a distance from Thee.

June 23, 1906

When I see souls fall under temptation I feel my heart ache, and their unhappy lot draws tears from me, and not reproaches. I, myself, Lord, have been too near the edge of evil, and for too long have been in danger there, not to be filled with mercy for the weakness of others. I believe and trust that Thou hast preserved me from death, oh! divine Master. Many proofs have I had to support this hope. And yet, I feel so deeply my faults and imprudences, that it is only Thy mercy that can find aught in me to glory.

I am thrown into confusion at the thought of the merciful pity Thou hast shown to me. I should like to write the history of my soul, for such an account would redound to the glory of Thy supreme goodness. Oh! God; and to the humiliation of a creature unworthy of Thy predilection. I see myself so full of miseries that nothing can set me free but Thy boundless charity. May it inundate my soul, and grant the only wish of my whole being!

June 28, 1906

Last evening, for the first time I had a violent attack of blood-spitting which weakened me so much that I asked myself whether I could, possibly survive! This morning I was rather better, and, thank God, was able to celebrate holy Mass easily. I thought a good day's rest would set me to rights, but there seems no chance of that, and, really, I feel I must have some rest.

I am ordered to rest, and, that it may be as complete as possible, I am consigned to the Infirmary of the Monastery. As I entered it, I felt the chill impression that inevitably is connected with arrangements for the sick who are near death. But the peace and tranquillity reigning here around me, lead the thoughts naturally towards Thee, oh! God. I feel quite happy, and my only fear is lest I should be unable to celebrate the holy Mass. If, however, I should be forbidden to do so, I will submit from the bottom of my heart to all that is ordered for me. I remain so entirely in Thine Hands, oh! my divine Master, that I will not even think, beforehand, of what may be done, and what may happen to me. May my love for Thee, weak as it is, make all things turn to my good, that is to say, to Thy Glory in me.

A Benedictine Soul

Maltebrugge, July 14, 1906

I have been brought here, to be thoroughly taken care of and have been here since July 3rd. I have not been out of bed at all. When shall I leave it again? I cannot say Mass, and, though I receive Holy Communion every day, I feel the deprivation of Mass is a great loss of strength. It is true, my God, that Thou canst compensate for this loss, and give grace as it seems good to Thee. But I seem to lose strength, because I am strongly tempted, because my soul does not find Thee as easily as I did formerly, and that the blessed intimacy with Him Whom my soul has chosen as its only Well-Beloved, does not hold me back from the evil tendencies of my nature; so it seems to me!

Ah! well! my Lord, my merciful Master, my pitiful Father, I pray Thee to cast a look of love on my poor, sinful soul! Have pity on it, as upon a poor, weak child; as upon a fragile blossom exposed to all blasts, as upon a tender plant well-nigh buried under the wayside dust! Hear—oh! sweet Jesus, hear this prayer which comes from my heart like a cry that has been too long repressed! On my own part, I renounce over and over again, everything but Thyself alone. I make this act from the very bottom of my heart, and all my will turns to this yearning want of Thee. Grant that I may live by Thee, in Thee and for Thee, and that my soul may be closed to all but this intimate life with Thee. In a few minutes, most merciful God, I am going to Confession and I bring to Thee a soul full of sadness at having displeased Thee; full of faults—full of desires never again to know the shadow of a stain, and full of fear for the future. I draw in wickedness like air, and I would only breathe my Justice, Wisdom, and Love. I put all my trust in Thee, my Saviour, help me to love Thee.

Malta, July 15, 1906

My eyes are full of tears, and my heart is swollen with the grief that weighs upon it! How is it that we fall unceasingly into the mire of sin?

Is this a disposition of Thy merciful Providence, or is it a chastisement sent by Thy holy and adorable Justice, oh! God? How long shall I live in this sad state of desolation? I want to love Thee, oh! my God; but I tremble at the thought that my life may, perhaps, drag on for a long time yet, deprived of the joy of the only Love which I have chosen for its pivot.

Malta, August 15, 1906

To Thee, oh! my gentle and merciful Mother, I turn today, addressing Thee. The sun has risen, somewhat, on my sinful soul; but how feeble and weak that soul is! I had been dwelling on the hope of keeping Thy Feast by offering the Most holy Sacrifice. Our divine Master does not allow me to do so! And I adore His holy Will. I feel, personally, too unworthy to offer the Holy Mysteries, to be surprised that our Lord should deprive me of doing so. But I want to offer Thee something on this Feast. In Thine honour, oh! holy Virgin, I will labour to become as pure and modest as an angel; and I offer Thee this, as being the greatest desire of my Soul; but, also as a real sacrifice, for corrupt nature and the sinful flesh will make me have to struggle hard to attain to this end.

Oh! my beloved Mother, Refuge of sinners! Tell Thy divine Son—I entreat Thee with all my heart—tell Him that my will remains inseparably united forever to Him alone. I love nothing really except Him and Thyself. I long and weary to see that happy moment when Jesus will receive my poor soul and take it wholly into His adorable Hands. I love Thee, my good Mother,—but grant that I may every day increase in Thy love!

Malta, August 23

It is unlikely that I shall be able to return to Maredsous for October, and the coming back of the pupils.

Last entry in "God's Note-book."

IV

Selected Letters

*In order to draw nigh to God,
it is very important to convince oneself of the
principles that form the basis of the spiritual life.*

—"Letter," February 2, 1901

I

To a Fellow-Monk

Pax   *Louvain, September 9, 1901*

My very dear Brother,

    Our interview was the cause of more joy to myself, perhaps, than to you; and this, because I see the great wish of my soul is being worked out. That wish is, that you may be completely given up to Christ. I have promised Jesus, that, for our ordination to the priesthood, we shall both, you and I, be *completely* His. Will you be angry with me for having taken this liberty? If you are—take your revenge, by going even further yet: "Hoc solum certamen sit inter nos qui vincat alterum per caritatem." It is so wonderful to live with Christ, when love fills our soul, for we take the only Object of our love everywhere with us, and hold converse with Him at will; but this must be on certain conditions—you will see!—I wish you a very good Retreat!

    For many years the only resolution I make is to live closely united with Jesus,—that is to say—recollected in my soul. When you have got the habit of recollection, you will soon find Christ in you. At first, this practice is rather hard work; and I wish to help you by giving you all my affection in Christ, as well as the prayers you know of.

A Benedictine Soul

On your part, please help me, for I need help very much. When we love, we are so *urged* to love more and more, and, by oneself one can do nothing: "Frater qui adjuvatur a fratre, civitas fortis."

Pax   Abbey Mont Cesar, November 10, 1901

My very dear Brother,

The post is leaving for Rome, and I take this opportunity to send you a little word, as I would not miss the chance of getting news of you. I have heard nothing from you since I saw you last, when we parted full of fervour to walk in the steps of our Divine Master. I still feel the same enthusiasm and am urgently wishful not to linger on the way.

So no wonder if I want to know whether we keep step well together. This won't be difficult for you, because I go along but slowly: at times of enlightenment I congratulate myself on not going back! Let divine love work in us; that is the true motive of all action. To give ourselves up to that, is, indeed, to hang on to a safe and sure cogwheel which carries us along as if unaware, by the easiest and most desirable ways. Like all strong wheels, this one may graze and bruise a bit, here and there on a weak or too sensitive part. We call out; but the pain has passed, and we have made another step.

Pray for me, for I have to prepare for my solemn Profession next March. But I think about you, all the same, and do not forget our little compact. Let us make progress by helping each other. Think, then, how good it will be to live holily—that is to say, solely to please our good and beloved Saviour! This view enchants me and would make me seem too much of a chatterer, if it were not that I remember you wish to know what we do that is good.

We are doing the treatise *De Verbo Incarnato*, which is so much the more beautiful because it makes one enter so deeply into the knowledge of Christ, and consequently fosters and increases love.

To a Fellow-Monk

In moral theology we are on the Sacraments; in "*Canon Law, de Personis*"; in Hebrew—still rather halting at translation. All this is well in harmony with the Divine Office, which I appreciate better every day.

Now I leave you, after this little chat! I should love to tell you a thousand times over, how intensely I long to see you belong all to Christ—the Only Priceless Jewel that tempts us—our Well-Beloved! May our soul (so capable of understanding the need of love), remember that both you and I have but one want, and desire nothing else. Good will on our part will attract the action of God Himself. In Him I love you devotedly, as you know.

Pax   *Abbey Mont Cesar, November 21, 1901*

My very dear Brother,

I have this moment received your letter and had no hesitation in asking leave to answer it by return of post. How happy I am to be able to be of any comfort to you! Yes, write whenever you are suffering. I understand your pains so well—and, if strength and consolation return to you in writing to me, I hope that both will increase, when, for my part, I have put all your sorrows into the Sacred Heart of our merciful Saviour. Believe that I am with you in thought and in prayer, so that my true affection aims at sustaining you every moment.

Our Beloved Master does not wish you to be an infant always: "*Jam non simus parvuli fluctuantes*"; but "*Veritatem facientes in caritate, crescamus in Illo per omnia qui Caput est Christus.*"[85]

This "Truth which we must do," is the giving of ourselves fully to Christ, because the Truth teaches us that, outside of Him there is no Truth to be found, nor any way by which to walk to Life.

---

[85] Eph. IV, 14 and 15.

To "give oneself to Christ" can be stated practically as absolute renunciation of all that is known not to be good, and of all the evil that may lurk in the soul. It is a firm will to "seek nothing but God," whether in study, or prayer, or in permissible distractions. In so far as this act is simple in itself does its accomplishment demand generosity at the outset, and result in happiness when it is repeated as one goes on. Our Lord's wish for our sanctification is more ardent than our own, for this desire caused His Death; but just in proportion as we hesitate to break with every known fault—however small—do we refuse to admit Christ's claim upon us, and, prevent Him from making us saints: for He is our Sanctity and none else can be. Our cooperation consists in giving ourselves up utterly to Him. When the will is fully determined to renounce all evil, and this disposition perseveres; first, all subsequent falls, being due merely to our frailty, have the effect of strengthening us in humility and confidence in God; and afterwards, Christ takes us entirely to Himself, in so far as we have really given ourselves to Him: "Sic nos tu visita, sicut te colimus."

The divine operation begins to transform the soul: and the more perseveringly we hold ourselves in the Hands of our Lord, so much the more will Grace sanctify us.

In the spiritual life there are two principles which are the very key of Heaven, and which flow, the one from the other.

I.—*We are holy, in the measure of our participation in the Sanctity of Christ.* Apart from Him there is no salvation. The problem of our sanctification is summed up in finding the means of sharing most abundantly in the holiness of Christ. The second principle shows us this means:

II.—*Christ acts in our regard as we act towards Him.* If we give ourselves up entirely to Him, He gives Himself fully, and thus

To a Fellow-Monk

we become holy. If we refuse, or hold back anything, He withholds His action, almost in spite of Himself—so long as we refuse Him—perhaps forever!

St. Paul teaches us the first axiom: "Unicuique nostrum data est gratia secundum mensuram donationis Christi,"[86] (To every one of us is given grace, according to the measure of the giving of Christ,) and Jesus Christ Himself teaches us the second: "In qua mensura mensi fueritis, remetietur vobis."[87] (With the same measure that you shall mete withal, it shall be measured to you again.)

My ambition, dearest Brother, is to see you entirely given up to Jesus-Christ—*All for Jesus*—for the glory and good pleasure of our dear Lord are so near to my heart; and you, yourself, will find happiness and joy beyond understanding—because infinite!

Be of good courage, then "Viriliter age et confitetur cor tuum, et sustine Dominum."[88] (Do manfully, and let your heart be strengthened, all ye that hope in the Lord.)

I am always very near to you, and Jesus is within you! Do I write at too great length? I want to imbue you with the doctrine with which our good Father Abbot feeds our souls, so that you may take it in deeply. You must make up by meditation for what it is impossible to say in a letter— always too short, on these subjects. Tell me, before long, what you think about all this; and, above all, let me hear that your dear soul has regained its peace. I want it to become a very warm little nest for Jesus; that is why I pour out all my affection for you, so that it may bring you the unction that love breathes—if only a little.

---

[86] Eph. IV, 7.
[87] St. Luke, VI, 38.
[88] Psalm XXX, 25.

Think of Mary, Consoler of the afflicted. She loves us so much that in leaving you now, I can say nothing better than that it is in Her I embrace and love you!

P.S. I advise you to meditate—and 1000 times, if possible—on the Epistle to the Ephesians—specially chapters I, II, IV.

Pax   *Abbey of Mont Cesar, January 7, 1902*

Very dear Brother,

I end my list of Christmas and New Year letters by this to you. Don't grumble at this—did not Our Lord Himself keep His last discourse for His best friends?

And first I must tell you the joy your letter gave me—only noticing one thing—for of itself your letter is enough. You wish; nay, "*You aspire to belong to God alone.*" There lies the whole thing: it is the germ of love. It is a need which day by day will become keener in your soul. May it go so far as entirely to consume it. Never mind how long this will take, but foster and cherish the tiny flame of love with jealous care, for therein lies the spark which causes the immense conflagration; and, some fine day, it will flare up.

A thousand times I would repeat to you, dear Brother, that we must give ourselves up to the love of Christ, because love brings all good to the soul. He who loves Jesus possesses in himself the Father, the Son and the Holy Ghost, as St. John's Gospel tells us, "If any man love Me… my Father will love him, and we will make our abode with him…and the Father shall give you another Paraclete that He may abide with you forever—the Spirit of Truth." *Si quis diligit me…et Pater meus diliget eum, et ad eum veniemus, et mansionem apud eum faciemus…et alium Paraclitum dabit vobis ut maneat vobiscum in aeternum…Spiritum veritatis.*[89]

---

[89] St. John, XIV, 23-16.

To a Fellow-Monk

In this we see a beginning of heaven on earth. Then again: "Qui diliget me...et ego diligam eum et manifestabo ei meipsum." He that loveth Me, I will love him and will manifest myself to him.[90] Now the manifestation of Christ to the soul is the greatest grace that we can desire; it is the beginning of the perfect union of the Bridegroom with the Bride.

Our part, then, is reduced to very little—to love and to wait, whilst doing the Will of God. This is an easy part, and sweet, for there is no bitterness save in constraint; love does not need laws, because its zeal runs on ahead, and farther than the law. Law fixes a standard beyond which no man may go.

Moreover,—I feel that love is the portion of our hearts. I see that yours longs to be satisfied with this living water. The world and the devil wish to quench your thirst with a drink, very sweet, indeed—but one that leaves a stain forever on the purity of the soul, and would extinguish the flame that is so precious, and which is already beginning its good though consuming work in your soul. On the other hand, I feel that my soul wants to love; a thousand and more times, and is too little, and too narrow! Jesus then decided for me that He would never give me anything else to do but to love, whatever burden He may reserve for me later on....But enough! I must conclude in a telegraphic style; and if you don't like it, next time my heart shall say less, and general news find a larger place! You can have your choice! I embrace you in Jesus-Christ, our Well-Beloved, and our Treasure, and I love you, as you know.

---

[90] St. John, XIV, 21.

A Benedictine Soul

Pax   *Abbey of Mont Cesar, April 6, 1902*

My very dear Brother,

There is just one page[91] left for me! Is that enough? I ask myself before deciding whether I will fill it....I decide to do so, as probably L...has written for your *ears*, and left it to me to speak only to your *heart*. Thus I am not required to send news. It is a long while since I heard from you. However, to speak frankly, I have been told that you are busy over a host of useless things—and I say to myself—*well*: provided they do not turn him away from speaking familiarly with Jesus, or—at least—do not keep him from seeking the Company of Jesus.

I feel so strongly, dear Brother, that it is to the love of Christ, and to Him alone, that you will give all the force of love of which you are capable, and that thus, only, the enthusiasm which you have will grow and increase with age. That enthusiasm is as fresh as youth, fragrant as a flower—warm as a flame of fire;—but it is not enough merely to keep it as it is; it must be made to grow and expand to its full capacity. This work of preservation and growth only operates in the degree in which we unite our souls to Christ, and direct the fullness of our strength to Him.

Ah! I want to say, and to repeat over and over to you, how entirely this truth absorbs and convinces me, perhaps you will catch the enthusiasm! If you only want to have a heart near you that is in true sympathy with your own, forget that you live in Rome, and I at Louvain: remember that, poor as it is, I offer you the poor little solitude of my soul, so that the contact with the fire with which our divine Spouse warms me, may take captive your energies, which you so lightly allow to escape! What will you say to all this, my good Brother? I should

---

[91] Written on the 4th page of a letter from another Brother.

To a Fellow-Monk

feel to have taken too great liberties if you, yourself, had not opened your soul to me to such a degree that I could sound it to the depths. And, on my side I cannot and will not hide from you the ardour of the feelings which animate me towards God.

Certainly, this is too much already, and lest I exceed further, I must cease! These lines will tell you that I am yours devotedly in Christ.

Pax   *Abbey of Mont Cesar, November 1, 1902*

My dearest Brother,

Behold! You are a deacon! I have known it for some days, and would love to know what the Holy Spirit has said to you, and in what way He touched your soul!

You appreciate too well the happiness of ascending to the Altar, not to taste the intimate joys of the sacerdotal grace! We are ministers of Christ. He has chosen us, and begins that work in us which will be completed on the day when we shall be ordained to the priesthood. Do not forget, my beloved Brother, that we have left the ranks of *servants* of Christ, to become the *friends* of His divine Heart. He invites us to live in intimate friendship with Him.

Oh! how intensely I feel the need of living a life hidden in our only and well-beloved Master!—and *you* want it too—don't you? For Jesus-Christ Alone is holy, "Tu solus sanctus." To understand this truth, and to be thoroughly convinced of it, is, I believe, the root and foundation of the sanctification of the soul. If we take in, once for all, that in our Blessed Saviour the Source of all heavenly blessings is found, we attach ourselves, once for all and forever—to Jesus-Christ.

For us, the thing is simple: obedience shows us where our divine Master is expecting us every moment. If we hasten thither, we shall be sure to find Him. The degree in which we possess the great treasure of union with our Lord, is marked by the degree of our Obedience; the degree of our obedience answers to the degree of intimacy existing between our soul, and the Heart of Jesus. All lies in this; to obey perfectly.

Now, obedience demands of us to be entirely submissive to Christ, not only in the person of our superiors, but more over in that of our brethren and in all events and circumstances; and this virtue grows even to the perfection of identifying our paltry sentiments with the most holy sentiments of Christ.

Ah! yes, only what God wills and loves is any good! and we ourselves are only good or holy in so far as we love the holy Will of God! That is really what matters to us, and what we must have, dearest Brother. I know your opinion as to this, and it agrees with my own.

This little chat seems to bring you back among us: in a serious way, perhaps, but, I believe, not coldly. Pray for me, as I do for you. Let us live in close union of thought, affection, and interest with Him Who is the only Real Good of our souls. Just as I am ending my letter, I find a thousand more things to say to you. You will easily guess what they are!

Pax *Abbey of Mont César, May 17, 1903*

My dear Brother,

I will write to you more at length than you have been able to do to me, and this letter will take you for a few minutes out of the "icy deluge" in which your thesis for the doctorate is plunging you.

I should love to tell you, if I could, all the consolation it gives me to see your dear soul advancing resolutely in the way of holy and ardent love of Christ; for that way is very sure, very straight, full of joy and peace. It is the way of happiness, both now and forever.

You know, my good, dear Brother, that, together with you, I wish to travel on this way—cost whatever it shall—it smiles at us in the most attractive manner. Let us walk on then, with firm and trustful steps, for we follow after our divine Master. This year we shall follow Him to the heights of Calvary. I own to you that the Priesthood, which is generally, and justly represented under its honourable aspect and in all the extent of its sublime dignity, does not, truly, seem to me to be anything else than taking on oneself an immense task. This task is the same that Jesus-Christ deigned to take upon Himself through His immense love, but not without feeling fear at facing so complete a self-immolation. Thanks to God, we have not to choose our way, any more than our Blessed Saviour chose His. Like Him, we wish that the Divine Will may be done, which we freely embrace in every point. That is the reason why we shall become priests. But what would (without trust in God) inspire an overwhelming fear is, that to become a priest is not all. From that very moment, the crucifixion of self begins! Our Lord has already let me see a little of what has to be put to death in my poor soul, and it is anything but a cheering sight!

And then, when once immolated, if we are true priests we must remain immolated all our lives. I speak like this to you because these are my secret thoughts, inspired by the weakness of my soul; and I lay them simply before you—not because I want to damp your own ardent enthusiasm—it is not *that* effect they produce in me—but, rather, that the consciousness of sacrifice may incite us to follow Christ. Oh! yes, the consciousness that the battle exceeds our own strength, and the determined will to struggle valiantly, harmonise well with confidence in our Jesus, Who is, and Who alone is our strength.

As to news, I will tell you that all here are well and happy. In dogma we are at *De Sacramentis in Specie*; in exegesis, the Epistle to the Hebrews: in moral theology, the Pastoral and Encyclical *Rerum Novarum*.

A Benedictine Soul

Know, dear Brother, that I desire for you, and for myself, a very close union with the Beloved of our souls; to this end Jesus-Christ gives my soul the facility and the expansion to love yours—as you know!

II

To Another Brother

Pax   *Louvain, November 29, 1901*

My very dear Brother,

    A few words for you, too—even if only a tiny word—to wish you a holy Advent. Let us go on towards Christmas enthusiastically. I seem to find many changes in my poor soul since leaving you; the days have gone very quickly, and, (thanks to God alone) as they have passed, they have taught me more and more what it is to love. Love becomes a more pressing and imperious demand in proportion as the soul develops in charity. Love opens horizons previously unknown, it invades our whole being, and takes it prisoner. When will the happy day come, when charity shall have dominated our souls, crystallising and fixing them forever in God? In my thoughts I cannot put off that happy day until a distant future. No! our hearts must beat with such a vehement longing that it will force Jesus to realise our desires for His divine love. Let us be bold enough to hope to see a part, at least, of all this before Christmas comes!

    The Treatise *De Incarnatione* gives us ample food for spiritual contemplation. What is there more sublime than that Sacred Humanity of our Blessed Saviour, full of the gifts of nature and of grace, Home of light and love, where the soul may become enlightened and warmed; for, to unite ourselves to Jesus-Christ by love, is not only to give oneself to Him, but also to receive Him in His entirety, as one's own belonging, and to possess His riches.

Here I am at the end of my paper, without knowing what I have said to you...let us work hard to love much. Think of me at Mass, and offer me to God unreservedly. On my side, I give you all I possibly can, for I love you sincerely in Jesus-Christ.

Pax   *Abbey of Mont Cesar, December 26, 1901*

Dearest Brother,

I fly to you in thought on this occasion of celebrating the Birth of our Only Beloved...at the sight of this dear little Infant I find only one emotion in my soul, and that is the wish to correspond with the "immense charity of our God." *Propter nimiam caritatem!* He embraces our miserable nature, and raises it to Himself; He purifies and divinely adorns it. How can we tell of the outpouring of graces on that divine Infant in the Crib? We must contemplate Him in excess of love like the Prophet-king "diffusa est gratia in labiis tuis" as if God had not been able to keep back the outpouring of His eternal love "therefore I have anointed Thee,"[92] for to be united to God is to possess eternal glory, and nothing else. If that is true in our regard, how much more in that Humanity which is united to the Person of the Word! Certainly that outpouring is peculiarly Christ's own. He enjoys it "prae consortibus tuis," but it seems as if an ardent soul possesses itself of this dear little Saviour without leaving anything of such a Treasure! It places Him in its heart, disposing of and enjoying all His riches. And how many are the riches hidden in Jesus! "Myrrha et gutta et casia a vestimentis tuis a domibus eburneis."

---

[92] Ps. XLIV.

To Another Brother

"Myrrh and stacte and cassia perfume Thy garments, from the ivory houses."[93] This garment, His holy Humanity is so full of graces that to be clothed upon with Christ is to disappear oneself under the abundance of celestial gifts, and to become pleasing to God, Who finds in us the "good odour" of His Well-Beloved Son; in short, to dwell with Jesus is the way to gain this blissful happiness which penetrates and inebriates all who have ever tasted of it.

Such is the effect of the eternal charity that God came down to bring us! Only an ardent faith can gauge the depths of the mysteries of the love of God for man. Those who try to penetrate it by the light of reason, only find that they know nothing of it, and look on it as folly: those who look at it in the light of love, penetrate it deeply, but, above all, they feel themselves drawn into that holy Way, where Christ has gone before. These are so many thoughts that fill my mind today; and you know well all that I mean, so that I can write to you freely, as you see.

Oh! yes, dearest Brother, together with you, I want nothing—I desire nothing, I long for nothing but to love as Jesus does, and with His Heart. There dwells all sanctity, for the love of Jesus has this especial property—that it is a transforming love....I must leave off—here are three whole pages!—only to tell you that God loves us, and to ask you to love Him wholly! Let us love each other tenderly, dearest Brother, for to love thus is to pray ardently.

Pax   *Abbey of Mont Cesar, April 1902*

Dearest Brother,

Your good prayers helped me to make an unreserved gift of myself on the day of my holy profession. May they now obtain for me to be

---

[93] Ps. XLIV, 9.

faithful. For, if it is easy to give oneself to God, it is difficult never to take oneself back! I feel supremely happy at being more closely bound to the Source of all good, the only and divine Object of all our desires! How can it be possible to love anything apart from Christ Jesus, when once it has been given to the soul to drink of the chalice of His love?

To live in close union with his God, means for the creature supreme happiness and the height of perfection. Why, then, should he defer such happiness, until the moment when not to accept it means an eternity of suffering? It is true, these things are told us in books, over and over again, and I should find it strange to repeat them myself, if the interior conviction that God gives me, did not make me pen them without premeditation.

Oh! dearest Brother; let us pray that our good Master may give us practical knowledge of truths of which the theoretical evidence seems trivial, because it is divinely simple. Everyone thinks he loves, and so few love in reality.

Just now we are enjoying some peaceful days in vacation, and are troubled by no distracting noises nor by any extraordinary event to disturb the tranquillity of our life. Days pass like moments when it is like this! Time that is spent for God passes happily, and I have no wish to use my time in any other way.

Pax   *Abbey of Mont Cesar, October 8, 1902*

Dearest Brother,

You have left your Office: do you feel the change very much? I think not. Don't you feel that the more we advance, really, the more we feel that nothing is stable but Christ, and that in rooting ourselves in Him we acquire a great stability of life, notwithstanding all that may happen?

We have had a good Retreat. The divine Master made me understand the necessity of ever advancing in the way of union of the soul

To Another Brother

with His own Sacred Heart. Herein, indeed, lies the principle of our life, the condition of our spiritual fecundity, and, as a consequence, our sanctity. Let us give all to Jesus. I feel so strongly that He asks from us all that we do, whether of good or indifferent things; let us bring them all to Him, like grain that has not yet been winnowed. He will refine the harvest Himself, and will increase its value by reason of the confidence which inspires us. How simple, then, is perfection! And yet, where do people go to look for it? But there is nothing astonishing in that; unless we consider how mistakenly men rely upon their own human strength in supernatural things; and, too, how the simple understanding of true holiness is a very rare grace. I believe it is the precious Pearl of the Gospel. More and more, everything tends to convince me that all our efforts should be directed to repent of our sins and to try to perfect our faithfulness in following our divine Master very closely. When the soul is actually and generously given up to Jesus Christ, it can live in peace; it will feel that it goes rapidly towards God, for its Beloved is carrying it. One word is enough to include everything—to love. Oh! dearest Brother, what admirable fruit does that soul bring forth that is animated by love! So well does that virtue fill the heart that it excludes the elements of corruption. Let us then make great and good use of charity, if we wish to remain close by our Saviour's side.

I speak to you quite freely of my poor little soul's desires, for you will better know the need I have of prayer, when you realise the goal which I long to reach. Alas! longing is not virtue! Let us pray more and more for each other, dearly loved Brother, for Christ has united us very Closely in the Furnace of His Sacred Heart. Live Mary! the Mother of our divine Saviour and our Mother too!

III

To His Mother

Pax   *Louvain, February 2, 1899*

My dearest Mamma,

    I have asked leave of our good Father Prior[94] to have a chat with you today, as we have a free day in honour of the Feast of the Purification, and I shall take advantage of it freely and at my ease, talking quite intimately. I always feel drawn more nearly to our Good Master when I can speak openly of Him with a soul equally attracted by divine Love, and able to understand what I mean.

    I want to pour into your heart all the graces and lights which the holy Spirit gives me here in a thousand ways, so that you may share in the benefit, and, also, that what I miss through my own shortcomings, you may avail yourself of! Am I wrong, dearest Mamma, to take this liberty very respectfully? And, besides, I shall not make long tirades which require intellectual labour, as our Lord so far surpasses my poor faculty, that often, after much toil and fatigue it finds itself obliged to give in to the will. This will, by an act of love tends and aspires towards its God as He is, the Infinite Being, the Immense, the Eternal—so that it may embrace Him in all His perfection. Whilst

---

[94] Dom Columba Marmion.

the intelligence, when trying to know God, draws Him down to the level that it cannot pass, the will, when once it has started in pursuit of its only Good—can *will* Him without lessening Him, can love Him more every day, and can rest continually in Him. These thoughts inundate me just now. The soul is, at times, madly pressed to love, but it swims in supernatural peace, and remains in a state where, though it is famishing, yet it does not suffer from the pangs of hunger. Whilst burning with the desire to possess its Beloved, it feels an assurance that it is lost in Him, for at every moment it fulfils the wishes of its Master, loving only, in these very wishes, the infinitely holy Cause from Which they emanate.

There lies the mystery of divine Love; it is, as it were, with the marvellous Mystery of the Eucharist which satisfies fully at the same time that it makes us hunger more keenly,—as we have the happiness of knowing!

It seems to me, dear Good Mamma, that we could lead a holy life in giving ourselves up unreservedly to our dear Jesus, without ever praying to Him for anything else but to know His Will, and to ask that It may be done—without doing anything beyond fulfilling His orders. Don't you agree with me that my view is a good one? But for some time I have noticed that the formal orders are not the most numerous. The holy Spirit speaks often to the soul that seeks Him and points out clearly how to act when in doubt. My deep conviction is that here below our only real regret ought to be that we are not faithful enough.

Is my letter too long? When once I begin about this, I might tire you out before I should come to an end! It is true, I only go on thus when writing to Mamma, who understands these things and who bears with me patiently if I overstep the bounds of discretion. Be sure and warn me, if I do this. Even now, I have to leave off without knowing whether I have said all I wanted to say—please understand all that I have left out, in the love that unites us to our Master.

To His Mother

I embrace you, as well as my dear Papa, with all my heart. Bless me, dearest Mamma; you know how much I love you in our Lord. I add to my letter a short sketch of our last conversation.

Principles of Spiritual Life[95]

In order to go to God, it is very important to convince oneself of the principles which form the basis of all spiritual life, for man acts by the will alone, and this *will* follows the intelligence faithfully.

In the degree that Truth enlightens us, Love inflames, when seeking holiness it is too often forgotten that God *Alone* is holy. He alone is holy, because He is *Holiness* itself. This Holiness consists in the fidelity with which He loves Himself perfectly, which is the immediate consequence of His own perfection. And our sanctity is nothing else but our love for God, love which is in proportion to the knowledge we have of God.[96]

Now, no one can give us this knowledge and this love but God Himself. It is God *Alone* Who can make us saints, since our sanctity is nothing else but a participation in that Holiness Which is God. But, according to the divine plan, we are chosen from all Eternity "ut essemus sancti et immaculati in conspectu Ejus."[97] Consequently, God *Wills* to communicate sanctity to us, and it belongs to Him to appoint the means and condition of that communication.

Christ is the Way for all: "Nemo venit ad Patrem nisi per me."[98] Christ, as God, contemplates in the Divine Essence, all that the holy Trinity decrees, not only in the general order of events, but also in all

---

[95] The pith of the following passages may be found by the reader of the ascetic teaching of Dom Marmion (Columba) in his "Christ the Life of the Soul."
[96] In proportion to the supernatural light of Faith, and not the knowledge by natural reason.
[97] "That we should be holy and unspotted in His sight." Eph., I, 4.
[98] "No man cometh to the Father but by Me." St. John. XIV, 6.

that regards each separate man, even to the details of his individual life. Our sanctity depends upon the execution in our souls of all that has been decreed for us. If this execution is faithful, we shall have attained to that degree of holiness which God willed to communicate to us, and we shall fully glorify the Lord, and our happiness will be complete. The only One who knows this mystery or, rather, this secret, invaluable to us, is the Word; and the Word has been made Flesh to work in us, and realize in our souls the designs which He intended. Thus, we have one only means of becoming holy, and that is, to give ourselves up entirely, fully and without reservation to the divine action. To wish to go by any other way is to try to attain the end by paths which we follow *without* the help of God, and, the further we go, the further we stray. And so we often see souls wearying themselves without profit, often getting discouraged, and even drawing back. If, however, they seek after their God with a right heart, they receive enlightenment from on high; little by little they change their method, and before long find themselves in the way which the Lord wills for them. One thing surprises them, and that is, the simplicity of sanctity; because it consists only in corresponding to the divine action, which alone *can* and *will* sanctify us. But what does that giving up of ourselves to Christ mean? It is the peaceful, entire, and *resolute* acceptation of the *whole* Will of God, leaving to Him to show It to us in everything, and on our side, fulfilling It with exact fidelity but without being scrupulous. From that moment, the soul must cast aside all human preoccupations which only hinder it and trouble it by giving birth to hesitations and such like thoughts.

God shows His Will in a different way to each individual soul. In general He makes it known by the Commandments and those of the Church, and by the duties of each one's special state. Then, in the practice of virtue; and, when the soul has become more closely united to Christ, by the Voice of the Holy Spirit, Whose language is only understood by a loving soul, and which is quickly recognised. This Voice of the Holy Spirit, without distinct words, inclines the soul to such or such a decision, when, in hesitation, it asks *before God*, but *by the light of its own reason*, where its duty lies? Whatever the results of its resolution may be, the soul before God has acted holily, and before men it has acted wisely in taking all the necessary precautions.

For the Religious, this obedience is a matter of every moment, since he has given himself into the hands of his superior.

This is what is meant by abandonment of self to Christ, the secret of our sanctification, the point to which all those come who draw near to God. Their obedience is sometimes very painful at first; but (as St. Benedict tells us in the Prologue to his holy Rule) if we go on faithfully and with generosity we shall "with unspeakable sweetness of love, run in the way of God's Commands."

IV

To One of His Sisters

Pax   *Abbey of Mont César, April 12, 1902*

My dear little sister,

Only a few words, to tell you what comes into my mind whenever I think of you. My heart's desire is that you shall be pleasing to our Lord. This sweet Master shows me how simple this is, and how a little soul that has never gone far astray, can attain to great perfection, as if in play.

In your heart, as in mine, our Lord has kindled a spark that we feel,—don't we? Well, the secret consists in one thing, which is, to watch well that we let the little Spark grow—never quenching or stifling its progress.

"Let us be very careful to guard against the little faults that hinder this flame; but we must do this without anxiety or minute searching. If the eye be attentive, it will see, or, rather, the flame itself will show what is getting in its way and will examine our conscience for It thus spares us the weariness of lingering too long over this: it shows us that we must attend to only one thing at a time, and this makes the work easy from the moment one has accustomed oneself to obey instantly as soon as love asks anything. Then, again, we must not stop to gaze too long at our poor soul in order to know it better and to work more at it. In my opinion, the sight of our own miseries is a sad spectacle, whilst fixing the eyes on our Lord's love, and the heart on being faithful to whatever He wants of us, fills the soul with consolation, peace, and purity because love consumes all its imperfections. Let us, then, attend only to love, since love is the happiness and the life of the soul, and the very essence of sanctity.

If you sympathise with me, dear little sister, you will very quickly feel that, which, for want of words, no one can express; I mean, the ineffable simplicity of holiness. Let us amuse ourselves, then, let us eat and sleep and work with great liberty of spirit, just easily—but let us do all this by love of our Lord. Everything will become delightful, as well to ourselves as to those who live with us.

That is the "little word" I want to write to you, my dear little Sister. I should wish you to let it sink deep into you, it is my life, and makes me very, very happy. And so, my affection for you wishes that you, too, may enjoy the same happiness. I kiss you, as I love you, in Jesus Christ.

Pax   *July 13, 1902*

My dear little Sister,

I have asked leave to write to you, because our souls, in drawing near to each other, stir up in one another a more ardent love of God.

Today is very fine, and we have just heard a lovely Mass in honour of the Feast of the Patronage of St. Benedict; I am bubbling over with joy, and in writing to you I want to share my joy with you. May both our hearts feel what a good and consoling thing it is to love our Lord. Cherish in your heart the flame of divine love, good little sister; it is quite as necessary in the world as in the cloister. Without it, we lead an entirely exterior life, ignoring our own soul and stifling it under the weight of material interests. Don't you feel, how, on the contrary, the life of a soul that is careful to shun a thousand little failings, and to establish the reign of Jesus-Christ within itself, is sweetly and profoundly intimate with Him? I spoke to you, one day, of the necessity of letting grace work: for grace is the great factor of perfection. This is, as I said then, the simple and infallible means of realizing great things in oneself. Let us oblige ourselves to avoid putting any obstacle to its divine operation: let us be minutely faithful in granting whatever little sacrifices grace may ask of us, and be animated by a zeal at once ardent and gentle, that will keep us all day on our guard against faults, will make us weep for our falls as soon as they happen, and, above all, may inspire us, weak though we be, with the utmost love and the desire to do, in union with that love, even the least things, whether agreeable or the contrary.

Everything is there—everything, I assure you, dear little sister—don't look elsewhere!—for my soul sees this very clearly, after having gone by ways more complicated, and less sure! By love our soul unites itself with Christ, and from that time forward it travels along gaily—no longer with sad looks, but running, singing, happy and joyful, following its Beloved, and telling Him of its love all the time, for thus it keeps up an intimate union with Jesus, even when He leads it by a way of suffering and humiliation!

The soul that really loves, accepts all from the Hands of its Good Master. It is enough that *He* gives it, to make the gift welcome.

You see, dear little sister, how this life that we must lead together, is very holy and full of consolation. Let us meet at the holy Table as often as possible; there we find strong Food, and the oftener we partake, far from causing disgust, the more it makes us hunger. When a soul communicates fervently, it does not grow weary of the Celestial Banquet, but finds it ever more and more full of delight.

I am not afraid to talk openly to you, my dear little sister, and heart to heart, for I know you are quick to feel that all this is more the overflowing of a loving heart, than the explanation of a system conceived in a dry way. I have many other things to tell you, and shall keep them for the moment when God allows us to meet together again. Here is just one of them. I should like to hear that you possess a New Testament in French. You would be able to read it every day, and so grow familiar with Christ's own teaching. Our dear Saviour has spoken with great simplicity, allowing all to have access to the Gospel, and this is too often left on one side for the sake of books of really very little value. You will see how beautiful the Gospels are—how deep, and how full of food for the soul that tastes and meditates on them. After having used these for spiritual food for one or two months, one feels it impossible to leave them, but prefers them to any other book. Happy is the soul who comes to this point, for it knows how to taste and enjoy the things of God. Choose a good edition, with translation and explanatory notes. It is good to have His own Life as it is good to have His Heart: it is one and the same thing. Enough! let us pray much for each other; I need prayers very much, for I am rapidly drawing near to the diaconate.

Your devoted brother, in Christ.

Pax September 27, 1902

My dearest Sister,

The vocation is nearly ended, and I am using one of the last free moments to write these few lines to you. They will, perhaps, give you as much pleasure as it gives me to write them, for I love to speak to those who understand that the love of Jesus-Christ creates profound intimacy in the soul. You know this, and begin to taste these joys: they ought to be the portion of every Christian, and not the exclusive privilege of religious only.

To One of His Sisters

All of us ought to lead that life of holiness, the model of which is set us by Jesus Christ, our divine Master. We have different occupations, it is true, but these are only means used by God to develop the interior life of the soul. That life does not change, it is the same for all of us and is naught else but the fire of charity, which our Lord wishes should inflame the world. A faithful Christian does not, himself, choose the means of acquiring this virtue; he listens to the Voice of God, and walks in the way by which he knows he is called. But, whether he follows Christ in the world, or whether he seeks Him in the cloister, he must live by charity.

I see that Life is growing in your soul, dear little Sister; do not forget, then, that the soul must be fed with solid food. Health is either robust or feeble, according to the kind of nourishment the body takes. As I told, you, after the holy Eucharist, and together with It, holy Scripture is the best of all food for the soul. Our Lord answered the devil, "not by bread alone does man live, but by every word that proceedeth from the Mouth of God."[99]

Well, the Scriptures are the Word of God, and to feed eagerly on these is to make a fount of living water spring up in one's soul, where one can drink at all times, in abundance, and at one's ease. To appreciate the word, the soul must feed on it with faith, that is to say, firmly believing that it issues from the Mouth of God, and is eternal Truth. If faith gives us the taste for this heavenly nourishment, charity makes us so fond of it, that we cannot endure any other again.

I am writing these thoughts in the solitude of our little cell, where I enjoy such complete peace that I love to have you share it with me: it is indeed true that we are happy in proportion as we enter into ourselves. Why do we hunt, about to find solitude, when it is so perfectly established in the depths of the soul? I think it is, because

---

[99] St. Math., IV, 6.

A Benedictine Soul

in order to come there, we must know the secret path of purity and love...and so few know this!

Let us love Jesus and His holy Mother very much, and one another in them.

Your devoted Brother.

V

To One of His Relations—A Nun

Pax   Abbey of Mont Cesar, December 2, 1900

My very dear Sister in Christ,

I think of you too much to allow this First Sunday in Advent to pass without celebrating it as a Feast with you—and I add to this letter some chosen extracts which I have copied for you, so that you may have a tangible proof of our union in Christ. How can we better fulfil Christ's wish than by loving, and seeking to be one in Him, as He asked of the Father, and also His precept to "abide in His love"?

For some time I have felt it was not enough merely to pour out to one another all the tenderness that our hearts are feeling in regard to Him Who is the One and only Object of our love: our minds also should mutually communicate the lights with which the Holy Spirit illuminates them, He Who is the "*dulcis hospes animae*," so that our wills may be stimulated by these, and more strongly attached to our Sweetest Saviour. Is it not true that there are moments when God deigns to dispose our poor intelligences to perceive some little glimpse of Himself, and that then we find ourselves overflowing with enthusiasm? One is confounded to see oneself called to contemplate the Divine Essence face to face! Ah! my well-beloved sister! I know how filled we are with these thoughts—and now, above all—when the Liturgy gives us such beautiful teaching, day by day.

The soul leaps in our body of death, as St. John the Baptist in his mother's womb, when we give ourselves up to the contemplation of the Mystery whose accomplishment we are expecting! Think, then, that the *Dei Sapientia*, that Word, Who from all eternity is the Wisdom of the Father, willed to come and restore the work of His Hands; that work, fashioned by Infinite Wisdom, and shamefully destroyed by man. With confidant boldness we cry to the Eternal Father angered by our iniquities, and we ask Him to send that Word, in Whom He is well pleased, "Emitte Sapientiam de coelis sanctis tuis, et a sede magnitudinis tuae,"[100] and then, *Angelus Domini nuntiavit Mariae, et concepit de Spiritu Sancto*, and all for love of us! Oh! dearest Sister, let us cast ourselves down before the Virgin, and, with the eyes of faith and love adore in her Womb the object of our love, our divine Saviour, *Dominus Justus noster*. I want, at every moment of this blessed season together with you to breathe out love to this good Master, who gives us Life. Being one with the Father, Christ is, like Him, the purely Eternal Act, possessing in Himself, in His immutability and His simplicity, all the reason of His Being, and His own infinite Beatitude.

Now, this beloved Saviour tells us in what His life consists; "*Vita in voluntate Ejus*,"[101] and by what food it is sustained "*Cibus meus est ut faciam voluntatem Patris mei*."[102] Let us feed on this sustenance, which, in scriptural language, makes us "as Gods."[103] We! who are but poor and feeble creatures, ever changing, and not knowing how

---

[100] "Send her out of thy holy heaven and from the throne of thy Majesty." Sap. IX, 10.
[101] "Life in His good will." Ps. XXIX, 6.
[102] "My meat is to do the will of Him that sent Me." St. John, IV, 34.
[103] Ps. LXXXIX, 6.

To One of His Relations—A Nun

to bind ourselves to the Supreme Good, we shall be made sharers in the immutability of our God.[104] We shall be enabled, even here below where all is transitory, to establish ourselves in that divine Eternity which, having neither beginning nor end, can have no "shadow of turning," and possesses itself *"tota simul."*

We shall acquire this stability in the measure we give ourselves up to Obedience, utterly and entirely into the Hands of our only Spouse. Every day I feel more and more, that I want nothing else but this, and I wish it with you, as you well know. You tell me not to wish to run too quickly; I accept the advice, unreservedly; I have laid it before Jesus, Who will take upon Himself to regulate the pace of my goings.

That's all....I have finished my Sunday spiritual reading, for all this is a chapter I find in my heart, of what the holy Spirit has been saying to me for the last two days; the chapter does not give the thoughts quite satisfactorily, but she who will read these lines knows the feelings of her correspondent, who has tried to tell of his love for our good Jesus. Goodbye, till Christmas, dear and good sister in Christ, and then, we must love the divine Infant better.

Let us keep close to Mary, who purifies us before His Birth, as He did St. John Baptist. Let us love as Jesus wishes, with an unlimited love because it is all for God.

Pax   *Easter Sunday, April 7, 1901*

My first outpouring of Paschal joy must be to you, dearest sister; and it is a very calm joy; incredibly calm for Easter Day!

Jesus puts into my heart what I wish tor you, as for myself—which is, to think of nothing but Heaven. At this moment I feel this very strongly. On one side I consider the glorious Mystery we are

---

[104] Eph. III, 6.

celebrating, whilst on the other I see myself all surrounded and penetrated by many miseries, and I feel keenly the need of lifting myself up with Christ above this world! I have to be satisfied to do it in desire whilst awaiting the blessed reality; but *"habentes pontificem magnum qui penetravit cœlos, Jesum Filium Dei, teneamus confessionem."*[105]

Yes. I hold on firmly forever to the Faith we profess! You'll think me too grave for such a Day: never mind—it doesn't matter if you don't read it, but I feel the need to talk thus with you, and it is extremely sweet to do so—as I shall with Jesus—it is recreation after Lent. I cannot tell you how much good it does me to show my poor soul to its innermost depths to some one who understands it. Why should I trouble that you must, at the same time, see so much that is vile! I remember with great joy the Holy Week of last year. I kept it among you all—and the first *Alleluia* was shared by us. However, it was really the same this year, notwithstanding the distance that separates us. Oh! how happy we are, my good sister! I speak to you now in great peace; and peace that is at once interior and exterior, and which is the delight of my soul! I hear from afar, the noise of a horrid little "round-about" at the other side of the rampart, but I cannot see it, as our windows are too high up: that hurdy-gurdy row throws into relief the tranquillity of our dear little cell, and the happiness there is in the repose of talking to you! Whilst these people are turning dizzily around!

You know we have vacation now; the exams are over and I don't know with what result, for nothing has been said to me about it, and I am always "out," when left to my own surmises. For my own part, I am pleased with the past term, in the sense that dogma always feeds my soul. The treatise on the Holy Trinity is admirable! It seems to

---

[105] "Having a great High Priest that hath passed into the heavens, Jesus the Son of God, let us hold fast our confession." Heb. IV, iv.

To One of His Relations—A Nun

me that nothing can surpass in sublimity the contemplation of the adorable Trinity in one Essence, knowing and loving Itself in such a way that that Intelligence, that Knowledge and that Love subsist individually in the Persons that are distinguished from each other by nothing outside of their mutual relations to one another. How exquisite it is to think that each one of these Divine Persons exists only in as much as It is related to each of the Others, and that It cannot exist by Itself. I do not know whether these beautiful thoughts impress you...in order to penetrate them they require very serious consideration. This thought, above all, thrills me, that the only Reason for the being of the Son, is the Father.

And we also are begotten—even we!—by this Heavenly Father, and consequently belong quite entirely to Him—*Deo gratias*! dear Sister!

During these few days of vacation, I intend to go again through the Treatise *De Deo Uno*, and give some study to the holy Scriptures: just at present I am in the Epistle to the Hebrews.

During the Watch at night between the Thursday and Friday in Holy Week, I stayed close to our good Jesus, in your name and in that of our dear Father Prior,[106] whilst meditating on the discourse of our Lord, after the Last Supper.

We need not to repeat the same thing twice—I want to love *very much*; so I have taken Jesus as Model. In Him I love you, as you know.

Louvain, April 22, 1901

Dearest Sister in Christ,

Your letter rejoices me, as all our talks together formerly did, and if I write so soon to you again, it is not only to thank you, but also

---

[106] Dom Columba Marmion.

to spend a few peaceful, happy moments before the opening of the Classes. Don't think that all moments are not "peaceful" and "happy" to me—you will understand what I mean!

Since yesterday, I have begun to be an "old abba" of 21!! In people's eyes I am a man, but those who can see into my *heart*, find that I am but a naughty Baby, who, as Father Prior said yesterday, in commending me to the prayers of the Community, is a Baby who has just "broken his bottle"! And now, at last, entering on riper age, I understand it to mean; "rooted and grounded in charity."[107]

The only great want I feel is this—I want to love: not only *amore*, but *diligere*. "I love Thee, oh! my God," this is what I could say, over and over again ten thousand times.—Till you would be tired of listening!—and, even then, I should not think I had said it often enough. I want to be a man,—but, like you—I long to keep a childlike tenderness towards our only Beloved. We must cherish Him together—our Best of Masters!—and seek such intimacy with Him that we may ever lavish on Him our respectful caresses.

Isn't it delightful, now that all Nature is waking up, to walk and think more and more of the Goodness of God, talking familiarly with Jesus Whom we carry in our hearts? I lie in wait for the chance of laying my head on the Breast of our Beloved, never against to withdraw it! Thank you for the good share you gave me in your prayers on Holy Thursday. Don't you find that after a long time of Adoration in which you have done nothing else but look at Him, you feel stronger—and that, truly, there is nothing to keep us here—below, any longer?

I have nearly gone through the Treatise *De Uno Deo* again....It is very fine; but what I want, is to possess, as much as possible, one single idea under which I can contemplate God better. God is simple, without distinction (as we shall see Him when we go to Heaven), and

---

[107] Eph. III, 17.

To One of His Relations—A Nun

that is why, here, more than anywhere else, synthesis is so desirable. It cannot fail, because it exists in reality in the Divine Essence, but our intelligence is too limited to be able to take it in. I would wish to see, at one view, all that is meant by the *actus purus*; Essence that moves by its own power, Intelligent, All-knowing and Almighty "*quaecumque voluit fecit.*" Nothing in God seems greater or grander that this Almightiness, which is really, not distinct from the Will, and Whose effects are infinitely good, since, when He wills, God can only will for Himself.

But I must wait till the end of the Treatise on the Trinity, to be able to form a true conception, as well as an analogy—I ought rather to say, to beg of God to enable me to do this.

The Infinite Essence of our God finds, so to say, its only "actualisation," in the Three Divine Persons. In These It completes Its operations, Its act of Intelligence and of Will.

When freed from the bonds of Nature, what joy it will be to plunge into the sublime depths of the Divinity! I do not like treating these studies as metaphysical speculations, they approach too nearly to prayer. You agree with me here—don't you? Let us go, then, together, to seek Divine Love there, where it burns most hotly—that is, in the Charity of the Holy Spirit, Who, in uniting us with the Incarnate Word, leads us by Him to the Eternal Father, before Whom we shall be holy and immaculate for all eternity. I am getting lost—happily I see this, in time!

Last week we were at Villers—you know those ruins—I spare you all comments—subjective—mystical—architectural and others!

Scold me for this endless scribbling—if I had not written it to you, I should have gushed it all out into "God's Note-book," for my soul needs to tell God that I love Him, or, at least, that I want to love Him. Thanks for good prayers. You know what love I have for you in our Only Beloved.

Your poor little brother, who is affectionately faithful.

A Benedictine Soul

Pax   *Abbey of Mont César, October 7, 1901*

You probably are expecting to know my impressions of our Retreat, and I tell you, with restrained joy and enthusiasm. Our Beloved has greatly enlightened me during these days of Benediction; less, it seems to me, by the instructions given us so carefully, than by the union of my poor soul with His. He spoke to me eloquently of charity. I thought myself already convinced of the need of loving, and now I feel more how vast is the precept of charity. Until now, I was satisfied in a way by the first part of the precept, and had not gone very deeply into the second, the *mandatum novum*.

As to loving God—I had been struck by the thought that man is, or ought to be, nothing but love. Every being possesses the same nature as its end; and since our end is charity, *Deus caritas est*, a man who is truly man, is necessarily love. And, if he is "rooted and grounded in divine charity," all his faculties, drawing their life and their strength from that same Root, must produce good fruit, and contribute in developing Christ in him; *"per omnia crescamus in Illo qui est caput Christus."*[108]

This thought greatly simplifies, if it is possible, the life of my soul, for it makes it easier to adhere to our Lord, and to fix one's eyes upon Him, rather than to follow the different movements of nature. To rectify the principle is to prepare good conclusions.

Whilst, as to charity to our neighbour, one thing was shown me clearly, and that is, that in the interior life the soul cannot withdraw itself from the surrounding world in order to love Christ alone, *"omne animal diligit simile sibi, sic et homo proximum sibi."*[109] If the principle in created beings of the same nature be true, it verifies itself in the Divine Nature. The Persons of the adorable Trinity mutually

---

[108] "In all things that we may grow up in Him who is the Head, even Christ." Eph. IV, 15.
[109] Briefly, we all love what is like ourselves.

To One of His Relations—A Nun

love each other infinitely because They are but one and the same Essence. How can we, then, who are all participaters in the divine Nature, be otherwise than united in one love, a love so intense as to banish egoism from amongst us, as amongst the Persons of the Most Holy Trinity?

All these reasonings are not necessary to make our dealings with others sweet and courteous. But it is not always so easy to bend one's will and understanding to those of other people. I wish, however, to attain to this, and this is my resolution.

When once one has well made up one's mind, it is only the "beginnings that are difficult"; for, from the moment our Blessed Lord sees our goodwill, He will do all the rest. I will not refuse Jesus anything that love asks of me. You know how eloquent His Voice is; and besides, nothing can be more foolish than to lose the whole for the sake of a part. The love of Jesus is, indeed, *All*; the rest, whatever we may think of it, is negligible really, and even worthy of contempt, in comparison with our Sole Treasure. I feel very tranquil and fully decided to turn to the love of Christ and of the Blessed Virgin, which in my heart are the same; nor would I, for anything in the world, take a single step without resting on their Arms, and on the Heart of our Beloved. Nothing else matters to me. I wish to love madly! My will; my understanding; all that I have, may be crushed, but I resolve never to desert this only Good; our dear Jesus. Better still, perhaps, I feel it is He, Who will never desert me. We must please Jesus, and Him alone. This feeling results in my loving you—in Him—tenderly, as you know.

Pax   *"Pascha Nostrum immolatus est Christus,"* April 14, 1903
Very dear Sister in Christ,

The words I write at the head of this letter do not mean that I am going to give you a sermon, rest assured. But the moment I begin to address you finds me so deeply penetrated by the need for God, that I am tempted to shut myself up in the interior silence of a conversation with the Beloved Master. More and more I feel that nothing—neither reading nor any other devout exercise, absolutely *nothing*—is more profitable to the soul, than a simple contact with God. But to converse with you, my dear Sister, is not to withdraw from that contact, but rather, it draws me closer, since I only know and love your soul in the holy love of God.

Now, tell me—don't you, too, find (perhaps more than I do), that there are times when our Divine Master presses our souls to love Him even more than usual, and seems—so to say—to be satisfied with awakening these desires? One must hope that these desires are but the advanced guard of true love. It is better to feel these things than to talk of them; still, when they happen, another need arises, and that is the need of pouring them out. It is very seldom that I can do this, except into the adorable Heart of our divine Saviour. But He eludes me so! Still!

I should love to know Him as a real Friend, as He is—and no more merely as the distant Object of all our loves. He is beginning to do this for me,—but He goes very slowly, considering the distance I have yet to travel.

I have no news from house, but I do not complain of the perfect solitude I am left in. I love them all more and more perhaps without their being fully aware of it, and wish only that I may live perfectly united with Christ. In Him, one finds *All*. I leave you, dearest Sister. Be so kind as to think of me in your prayers, as well as all those to be ordained with me. Thus, you will be forming Priests, which is a great work.

You know all the affection that unites me to you, in our Saviour.

To One of His Relations—A Nun

Pax *Maredsous, November 21, 1905*

Very dear Sister,

I had counted on asking leave to go and see you on your Feast, but the good God holds me here by the throat. The malady is nearly gone, however. I have never wished to take my neck out from under the yoke, and I prefer not to put my share of the burden on my good brethren who are already over-laden. All this is to tell you why my visit is only by letter, but it loses nothing of fraternal cordiality. I have become such a mundane man that I felt I must rack my brains to send you a few ascetic phrases! You know, these queer ideas don't go very deep.

Now I formulate once again—very simply and intensely—the wish, ever renewed as the thing we aim at, that we may love our good God very much. And, if I wish for you this precious treasure of divine love under the most tangible aspect possible, considering the weakness of our nature, I would pray Our Lord to foster the growth toward our Good, in your heart, as in my own.

When the soul has come to know itself in the midst of the spiritual life and has been able, with a light heart to travel by leaps and bounds along the way during some time, can anything else (I ask myself) be left in her, than a great, simple need for God? This is what I shall ask for you, to the degree that forms saints. For the rest, however low we are in the road of ascent towards perfection, and in however painful a state we may find ourselves, it is always possible to protest that we desire nothing but God alone. This is childlike simplicity.

Now—a happy Feast to you! I shall be with you in thought all that day, and you will do well to give a tiny scrap of thought to your little Brother, who feels great need of support.

Till we meet again! The true affection I bear you is a great strength to me. That is why our Divine Master keeps it growing and growing.

VI

Thoughts and Letters of Dom Pius

May 20, 1906

I do not know how to express myself openly: and I mistrust others too much to do so.

You dread, o little flower, and with reason, to grow in full daylight. The hurricane would soon annihilate your frail existence, and blow away all your fragrance. But why, tell me, why should you fear to display your charms in solitude? No one would see you, except a soul that is enamoured of the beauties of nature, and thirsting as you do, yourself, for a peaceful and solitary life.

There! lift up your head again, expand your petals and shed forth your perfume. Show how God makes you beautiful, sing, after your own fashion your love for Him—your enthusiasm—and all that your little opened chalice contains.

—And why? Everything passes away! The flower soon fades—Its petals fall—and forever! Is there no illusion in all that?

—Yes, certainly. But provided that it fades for God, it is an illusion that is holy and becoming less and less of an illusion each day, because it is always being transformed in the divine Reality.

Oh! timid little flower! Live alone, in the bosom of the great solitary woods! He alone follows who feels the same!

Oh! sweet little flower? Grow, grow tall, delicate and tender. May the mosses protect your slender stalk! May the refreshing dew fall on your little head! And may you remain pure and beautiful; as God created thee!

Maltebrugge, August 25, 1906

My dear M.,

Are we yet in the spirit of the Old Law, that we write with increasingly long intervals, like those who gave "a tooth for a tooth"? In your letter of the 6th of August (!) you make excuses for writing so tardily, and twenty days after I reply. But I excuse myself because I wished to send you the report asked for by your dear Mother.

The absence of my Parents, and other reasons beside, prevented me from speaking of that affair to my mother. But today my mother gave me a most practical solution; the commission to send a little Manual of examination. Forgive that it is a trifle worn: I do not like to delay my letter—already behindhand—by looking for another copy.

You thank me for your nomination as president of our Conference. You must only thank our Lord for that; but you must know that to thank Him for it, means to say that you are glad to be able to devote and sacrifice yourself: devotion to the poor demanding an equable mind and an unfailing charity—self-sacrifice includes setting a good example to all around.

We will sacrifice ourselves together from the beginning of the year: on my part certainly in a way that is the most painful possible: and on your part painful too, because of your affection for me. In fact, I very much doubt that I shall be able to go back in October to Maredsous. Still, I am pretty well; I got up yesterday, but the doctors and my Superiors want to make a thorough cure. I will talk with you by my pen instead of with my tongue, and prayer will unite us. Pray for me I shall be very grateful. Let us love to submit always to the Divine Will: often It causes separation from a material point of view, but always unites hearts that are grounded in It.

As to you, my dear M...you have opened your heart and your soul to me. Although far away, yet, believe me, I always bear them in my affections. Remind your good father of me and give my respects to your mother. I will do as she wishes with regard to the reports on the Conference.

Yours devotedly.

Dom Pius de Hemptinne.

To One of His Relations—A Nun

Maltebrugge, October 16, 1906

My dear M.,

—We two live very much together; this is enough for a hundred excuses as to the long silence which is undesirably long! The memory of those who are absent is soon blotted out unless they place that memory in Him with Whom nothing is forgotten. And so, I find you in Him, because I have put you there—entirely and forever. So, I can meet you at any moment there, and love you all the more and with perfect freedom.

Nevertheless I love to read your letters, for your words make me feel you near me *alive*. I am delighted to hear good news of the School. You are rhetorician and at the head of your condisciples! Work hard at spreading a good spirit, above all in relations with the Fathers and Professors. A family spirit demands love and devotion on the part of superiors, and docility from the children, as well as devotedness in helping their superiors. But I am saying too much. Do your best with Flemish! what a man! I think Dom John could do you great good, if you will let him. I've still a thousand things to say to you, but I must leave off, and you must guess at all the rest—the conference of St. Vincent—all my poor people—and so on. I will send you the fruit of our labour (that of my Sister-Nurse and myself). Goodbye. May God ever keep you, that I may always meet you affectionately in Him.

Dom Pius de Hemptinne, O.S.B.

I forgot to give you news of myself. My health must be good, or I shouldn't have forgotten it! I am to get up next Thursday.

Appendix 1

Letter from the Countess de Hemptinne, mother of Dom Pius, in reply to the condolences sent by the President of the Conference of St. Vincent de Paul at Maredsous, of which Society Dom Pius had been Director.

Ghent, March 27, 1907

My dear Sir,

The kind letter you have written to me in my great sorrow, has touched me deeply....You write in such affectionate and appropriate terms of him whom it has pleased God to take from our love, that in re-reading your letter my tears flowed anew. The designs of Providence are inscrutable: God has cut short an existence in its early bloom, which seemed to promise a beautiful fruition. He allowed us to enjoy the sight of that lovely soul for so short a time, in order that, during a few days we might be instructed by the spectacle of such virtue—and then, so soon it was hidden from our eyes and torn from the love of our hearts....*Sursum corda!* Lift up your hearts!

He whom we love had given himself to God: we had consented to the sacrifice to the utmost extreme—even to death..."God so loved the world that He gave His only Son"...after that, can we complain of the bitterness of our grief? In heaven we shall understand why all things have been. In heaven, by the bright rays of faith we shall see and meet again those who have left this vale of tears in the Grace of God...."Left"—is not that too material an expression when one speaks of a soul? The soul that is purified and is in God, sees and knows those whom it has known and loved here below...the Gospel gives us this belief...and so my greatest comfort is to find and meet again in prayer my dearly-loved son.

Does he not love us better and more efficaciously in the eternal life, than he could ever do in the days of his mortal existence? Certainly, he sees in God his dear poor, for whom he loved to employ his leisure in sickness: in Him he continues to love those who were his companions in good works and will help to obtain for them the happiness he wished and longed for for them. I had thought to thank you in a few words for the tribute of sympathy and gratitude that you have rendered to the memory of my son—but when I write of him, my pen runs away with me.

Forgive the length of this letter and see in it the expression of the sympathy and gratitude inspired by your letter.

Countess Paul de Hemptinne.

Appendix II

In October 1922, the Abbey of Maredsous celebrated its fiftieth year of existence. At the fraternal Agapes which followed the religious ceremonies, His Eminence Cardinal Mercier, in dwelling on the past of the Monastery, recalled the memory of certain souls who had in particular embalmed the cloisters of Maredsous with the perfume of their virtues.

Among these, the eminent Prelate distinguished, the "Angelic" face of Dom Pius and declared before a numerous assembly that the cause of the young monk deserved to be introduced at Rome. The value of this opinion from such a witness can be understood.

Among many other favours obtained through the intercession of Dom Pius, we will give the following.

Morrone (Campotano), September 8, 1931

Very Reverend Father,

The echoes of the Life of Dom Pius de Hemptinne have reached even so far as to us, and have aroused—especially in my own soul—a great admiration and veneration for the saintly young monk.

And he has rewarded this devotion by obtaining for me from God a great grace, which I venture to acquaint your Reverence with in this letter.

A man who had been ill for a long time, and was near to death, had obstinately refused to receive the Sacraments: and would not endure the presence of a priest near him. His daughters being good christians had done all in their power to prevent their father from dying in that state, but all their efforts were unavailing.

I earnestly recommended the poor soul to Dom Pius, promising to celebrate Masses every year to obtain that God would deign to glorify on earth this illustrious son of Maredsous,—and the grace came.

Would to God that Jesus would add this beautiful jewel as one more precious stone, to the crown of Saints which encircle our holy Father St. Benedict's head.

I should be delighted if you would send me a photograph of Dom Pius and some small object which he used during his lifetime.

Receive, I beg you, Reverend Father, the assurance of my sincere respects and believe me yours devotedly in Jesus-Christ,

Jules Mastrogiacomo,
Priest Oblate, O. S. B.

About The Cenacle Press
at Silverstream Priory

An apostolate of the Benedictine monastery of Silverstream Priory in Ireland, the mission of The Cenacle Press can be summed up in four words: *Quis ostendit nobis bona*—who will show us good things (Psalm 4:6)? In an age of confusion, ugliness, and sin, our aim is to show something of the Highest Good to every reader who picks up our books. More specifically, we believe that the treasury of the centuries-old Benedictine tradition and the beauty of holiness which has characterized so many of its followers through the ages has something beneficial, worthwhile, and encouraging in it for every believer.

cenaclepress.com

Also available from The Cenacle Press at Silverstream Priory

Robert Hugh Benson
The King's Achievement
By What Authority
The Friendship of Christ
Confessions of a Convert
Papers of a Pariah
Christ in the Church

Blessed Columba Marmion OSB
Christ the Ideal of the Monk
Christ in His Mysteries
Words of Life On the Margin of the Missal

Dom Hubert Van Zeller OSB
Letters to A Soul
We Work While the Light Lasts
The Yoke of Divine Love

Dom Eugene Vandeur OSB
Hail Mary

Maurice Zundel
The Splendour of the Liturgy

Father Ryan T Sliwa
New Nazareth's In Us

Monks of Silverstream Priory
Dawn Tears, Spring Light, Rood Peace: Poems

cenaclepress.com

www.ingramcontent.com/pod-product-compliance
Lightning Source LLC
Chambersburg PA
CBHW021140080526
44588CB00008B/150